Why did the chicken cross the road?

and other hilarious jokes for kids!

Contents

Crazy as a coconut

⊙ What lies at the bottom of the sea and shakes?

🅰 A nervous wreck

☆✪☆✪☆✪☆✪☆

⊙ **How do you send a message in the woods?**

🅰 **By moss code**

☆✪☆✪☆✪☆✪☆

⊙ **What never gets wetter, no matter how much it rains?**

🅰 **The ocean!**

☆✪☆✪☆✪☆✪☆

Two silkworms decided to have a race. But, it ended in a tie.

☆✪☆✪☆✪☆✪☆

⊙ **Where do aliens keep their sandwiches?**

🅰 **In their launch box**

☆✪☆✪☆✪☆✪☆

Q Knock, knock!
Who's there?
Terry
Terry who?
turn over for answer!

Q What do mermaids have on their toast?

A Mermerlade

☆✪☆✪☆✪☆✪☆

Q What do monsters make with cars?

A Traffic jam!

☆✪☆✪☆✪☆✪☆

Q What bird can be heard during mealtimes?

A A swallow

☆✪☆✪☆✪☆✪☆

Q What's a flea's favourite way to travel?

A Itch-hiking

Q What happened when the cow jumped over the barbed wire fence?

A It was an udder catastrophe!

☆✪☆✪☆✪☆✪☆

Animal antics

⊙ What's striped and bouncy?

🅰 A tiger on a pogo stick!

☆✪☆✪☆✪☆✪☆

⊙ **What's the time when an elephant sits on your fence?**

🅰 **Time to get a new fence!**

☆✪☆✪☆✪☆✪☆

⊙ What's a pig's favourite ballet?

🅰 Swine Lake!

⊙ **What do you call a pig driving on the motorway?**

🅰 **A road hog**

☆✪☆✪☆✪☆✪☆

⊙ Which insect makes movies?

🅰 Stephen Speil-bug!

☆✪☆✪☆✪☆✪☆

⊙ **What's grey and red?**

🅰 **An embarrassed elephant**

☆✪☆✪☆✪☆✪☆

🅐 Terry-dactyl!

Ghoulishly funny

Q Why was the student vampire tired in the morning?

A Because he was up all night revising for his blood test!

☆✪☆✪☆✪☆✪☆

Q How do you fit twelve monsters in a biscuit tin?

A Take all the biscuits out first

Q Why are some monsters big and hairy?

A So you can tell them apart from gooseberries

☆✪☆✪☆✪☆✪☆

Q Why did the man call his pet monster Fog?

A Because it was thick and grey

☆✪☆✪☆✪☆✪☆

Q How do vampires keep their breath from smelling?

A They use extractor fangs

9

Doctor, Doctor

Doctor, Doctor, I've lost my memory

When did this happen?

When did what happen?

☆✪☆✪☆✪☆✪☆

Doctor, Doctor, I feel like a bee

Buzz off, I'm busy!

☆✪☆✪☆✪☆✪☆

Doctor, Doctor, I think I'm an electric eel

That's shocking news!

☆✪☆✪☆✪☆✪☆

Doctor, Doctor, I feel like a pair of curtains

Pull yourself together!

☆✪☆✪☆✪☆✪☆

Doctor, Doctor, everyone keeps ignoring me

Next please!

Slapstick

Q How does the Moon cut his hair?

A E-clipse it!

☆✪☆✪☆✪☆✪☆

Q Why do cows have bells?

A **Because their horns don't work**

☆✪☆✪☆✪☆✪☆

Q **What do you call a lion with a toothache?**

A **Rory**

☆✪☆✪☆✪☆✪☆

Mother: Why did you swallow the money I gave you?

Son: You said it was for my lunch.

☆✪☆✪☆✪☆✪☆

Q What happened to the dog that swallowed a firefly?

A It barked with de-light

☆✪☆✪☆✪☆✪☆

Q **What do people do in clock factories?**

A **They make faces all day**

☆✪☆✪☆✪☆✪☆

Bad boys

Q **Did you hear about the dizzy boy scout?**

A **He spent all his time doing good turns!**

☆✪☆✪☆✪☆✪☆

Gavin: Why does your brother wear a life jacket in bed?

Simon: Because he sleeps on a waterbed!

☆✪☆✪☆✪☆✪☆

When Terry proposed to his girlfriend she said, "I love the simple things in life, Terry, but I don't want one of them for a husband!"

Dan: My little brother's a real pain

Steve: It could be worse.

Dan: How's that?

Steve: He could be twins!

☆✪☆✪☆✪☆✪☆

Q **Why did the stupid boy wear a turtle-neck sweater?**

A **To hide his flea collar**

Good girls

Sarah: I'd buy that dog, but his legs are too short!

Jane: Too short? But, all four of them reach the floor.

☆✪☆✪☆✪☆✪☆

James: I call my girlfriend Peach.

John: Why, because she's beautiful?

James: No, she's got a heart of stone!

☆✪☆✪☆✪☆✪☆

When my girlfriend goes riding, she looks like part of the horse. When she gets down, she still looks like part of the horse!

☆✪☆✪☆✪☆✪☆

◉ **What did the zombie say when he got a letter from his girlfriend?**

🅐 **It's a dead letter day!**

☆✪☆✪☆✪☆✪☆

Mother: What do you mean, the school is haunted?

Daughter: Well, the headmaster kept talking about the school spirit.

☆✪☆✪☆✪☆✪☆

◉ **Why did the monster's girlfriend break up with him?**

🅐 **Because he had such a powerful crush on her**

Going bananas

⊙ How do you know when your dog has been naughty?

🅰 It leaves a poodle on the carpet

☆✪☆✪☆✪☆✪☆

⊙ **What's black and white and sleeps a lot?**

🅰 **A snooze-paper!**

☆✪☆✪☆✪☆✪☆

Robbie: Dad, can you write in the dark?

Father: I think so. What do you want me to write?

Robbie: Your name on my report card.

☆✪☆✪☆✪☆✪☆

⊙ **What breaks when you say it?**

🅰 **Silence**

☆✪☆✪☆✪☆✪☆

⊙ What goes tick, tock, woof?

🅰 A watch dog

☆✪☆✪☆✪☆✪☆

⊙ **Who writes nursery rhymes and squeezes oranges at the same time?**

🅰 **Mother Juice**

☆✪☆✪☆✪☆✪☆

Q What do you call a rodent with a sword?

A A Mouseketeer!

☆✪☆✪☆✪☆✪☆

Q What do you get if you cross a hedgehog with a giraffe?

A A long-necked toothbrush!

☆✪☆✪☆✪☆✪☆

Q Who is a dog's favourite comedian?

A Groucho Barks

☆✪☆✪☆✪☆✪☆

Q What was Camelot?

A A place where people parked their camels

☆✪☆✪☆✪☆✪☆

Q Why is a baseball team like fried fish?

A They both depend on the batter

Bonkers!

Waiter, this soup tastes funny

Then, why aren't you laughing?

☆✪☆✪☆✪☆✪☆

◉ **What's the fastest thing in water?**

🅰 **A motor-pike**

◉ **Why did the sword swallower swallow an umbrella?**

🅰 **He wanted to put something away for a rainy day**

☆✪☆✪☆✪☆✪☆

◉ Why did the lazy man want to work in a bakery?

🅰 So he could loaf around

☆✪☆✪☆✪☆✪☆

◉ **Which actor is always short of money?**

🅰 **Skint Eastwood**

☆✪☆✪☆✪☆✪☆

⊙ Who was the first underwater spy?

🅐 James Pond

☆✪☆✪☆✪☆✪☆

I'd tell you another joke about a pencil, but it doesn't have any point!

☆✪☆✪☆✪☆✪☆

"Quick, take the wheel," said the nervous driver.

"Why?"

"Because there's a tree coming straight for us!"

☆✪☆✪☆✪☆✪☆

Debbie: This match won't lig

Kate: That's funny, it did this n. ⌐.

☆✪☆✪☆✪☆✪☆

⊙ Why do idiots eat biscuits?

🅐 Because they're crackers!

☆✪☆✪☆✪☆✪☆

Q Knock, knock!
Who's there?
Arthur
Arthur who?
turn over for answer!

17

Hilarious history

⊙ Who designed Noah's ark?

Ⓐ His ark-itect!

☆✪☆✪☆✪☆✪☆

⊙ **What happened when the lion tamer put his head into the lion's mouth to see how many teeth he had?**

Ⓐ **The lion closed its mouth to see how many heads the lion tamer had!**

☆✪☆✪☆✪☆✪☆

Spanish explorers sailed round the world in a galleon. How many galleons did they get to the mile?

☆✪☆✪☆✪☆✪☆

⊙ What did the Sheriff of Nottingham say when Robin Hood fired at him?

Ⓐ "That was an arrow escape!"

☆✪☆✪☆✪☆✪☆

⊙ **Why did the Romans only build straight roads?**

Ⓐ **To stop their soldiers from going round the bend!**

☆✪☆✪☆✪☆✪☆

A Arthur more cookies in the jar?!

Mad world

Why did the atoms cross the road?

It was time to split

☆✪☆✪☆✪☆✪☆

On which side does a chicken have the most feathers?

The outside

What do you call a woman balancing a pint of beer on her head while playing pool?

Beatrix Potter!

☆✪☆✪☆✪☆✪☆

What part of a fish weighs the most?

The scales

☆✪☆✪☆✪☆✪☆

What do you call 20 rabbits moving backwards?

A receding hare line

Fit for fun

⊙ Why don't they build football stadiums in outer space?

Ⓐ Because there's no atmosphere!

☆✪☆✪☆✪☆✪☆

⊙ **Where do spiders play their FA Cup final?**

Ⓐ **Webley stadium!**

☆✪☆✪☆✪☆✪☆

⊙ **What is a frog's favourite sport?**

Ⓐ **Croak-vet!**

☆✪☆✪☆✪☆✪☆

Manager: I told you to lose some weight! What happened to your three-week diet?

Player: I finished it in three days!

☆✪☆✪☆✪☆✪☆

Manager: Twenty teams in the league and you lot finish bottom?

Captain: Well, it could have been worse.

Manager: How?

Captain: There could have been more teams in the league!

☆✪☆✪☆✪☆✪☆

⊙ **Where do footballers dance?**

Ⓐ **At a foot-ball!**

Q Why do managers take suitcases to away games?

A So they can pack their defence!

☆✪☆✪☆✪☆✪☆

Q **Why are football grounds odd?**

A **Because you can sit in the stands but you can't stand in the sits!**

☆✪☆✪☆✪☆✪☆

Q Where do religious school children go at lunchtime?

A To the prayground!

☆✪☆✪☆✪☆✪☆

Q **What's a tennis player's favourite city?**

A **Volley-wood!**

☆✪☆✪☆✪☆✪☆

Manager: Our new striker cost £10 million. I call him our wonder player.

Fan: Why's that?

Manager: Everytime he plays I wonder why I bothered to buy him!

Gag-tastic!

⊙ What do you call a bad lion tamer?

A Claude Bottom

☆✪☆✪☆✪☆✪☆

⊙ What do you get if you cross a pig with a centipede?

A Bacon and legs

☆✪☆✪☆✪☆✪☆

A Sunday school teacher was speaking to her class. Just before she dismissed them to go to church she asked them, "Why is it necessary to be quiet in church?" Little Billy shot up his hand and said, "Because people are sleeping!"

☆✪☆✪☆✪☆✪☆

Emma came home from her first day at school. Her mother asked, "Well, what did you learn today?" Emma replied, "Not enough. They want me to go back tomorrow!"

☆✪☆✪☆✪☆✪☆

⊙ What drink do frogs like?

A Croak-a-Cola

⊙ How can you tell if a ghost is flat?

A Use a spirit level

☆✪☆✪☆✪☆✪☆

Q Why did the man put all his money in the freezer?

A He wanted cold hard cash!

☆✪☆✪☆✪☆✪☆

Q **What does a policeman use when he arrests a pig?**

A **Ham-cuffs**

☆✪☆✪☆✪☆✪☆

Q What kind of button won't come undone?

A A belly button!

☆✪☆✪☆✪☆✪☆

Q **What do you do if your chair breaks?**

A **Call a chairman**

☆✪☆✪☆✪☆✪☆

Q How much do pirates pay for their earrings?

A A Buck-an-eer!

School daze

Pupil: What's this fly doing in my soup?

Dinner lady: The breast stroke!

☆✪☆✪☆✪☆✪☆

Teacher: What do we call the outer part of a tree?

Pupil: I don't know, Miss

Teacher: Bark, silly, bark!

Pupil: Woof, woof!

☆✪☆✪☆✪☆✪☆

Teacher: Smith, didn't you hear me call you?

Smith: Yes sir, but you told us never to answer back!

Q Why did the teacher put the lights on?

A Because the class was so dim!

☆✪☆✪☆✪☆✪☆

Teacher: When do you like school most?

Pupil: When it's closed!

Teacher: Where does your mother come from?

Pupil: Alaska!

Teacher: Don't worry, I'll ask her myself!

☆✪☆✪☆✪☆✪☆

Teacher: In the exam you will be allowed 30 minutes for each question.

Pupil: How long for the answers sir?

☆✪☆✪☆✪☆✪☆

Q When a teacher closes his eyes, why does it remind him of an empty classroom?

A Because there are no pupils to see!

☆✪☆✪☆✪☆✪☆

Teacher: If you had seven haystacks in one corner, five in another and two in another, how many would you have?

Pupil: One huge haystack!

☆✪☆✪☆✪☆✪☆

Q What tables don't you have to learn?

A Dinner tables!

☆✪☆✪☆✪☆✪☆

Teacher: What are you reading?

Pupil: I don't know.

Teacher: But you're reading aloud!

Pupil: But I wasn't listening!

Crazy as a coconut

Q **Why do fish live in saltwater?**

A **Because pepper makes them sneeze**

✩✪✩✪✩✪✩✪✩

Q What do sheep do on sunny days?

A Have a baa - baa - cue

✩✪✩✪✩✪✩✪✩

"Are you sure this money was lost?" the mother asked her son when he showed her the £10 note he'd found. "Of course I'm sure!" he said. "I even saw the lady looking for it!"

✩✪✩✪✩✪✩✪✩

Q **Why did the girl throw her butter out of the window?**

A She wanted to see a butterfly

✩✪✩✪✩✪✩✪✩

Q **Did you hear about the cross-eyed teacher?**

A **She couldn't control her pupils!**

What do you call...

- What do you call a man with a plank on his head?

- **A** Edward

☆✪☆✪☆✪☆✪☆

- **What do you call a man with a kilt on his head?**

- **A** **Scott**

☆✪☆✪☆✪☆✪☆

- **What do you call a man with a boat on his head?**

- **A** **Bob**

☆✪☆✪☆✪☆✪☆

- What do you call a man with a stamp on his head?

- **A** Frank

☆✪☆✪☆✪☆✪☆

- What do you call a woman with a tortoise on her head?

- **A** Shelley

☆✪☆✪☆✪☆✪☆

- **What do you call a man with a seagull on his head?**

- **A** **Cliff**

☆✪☆✪☆✪☆✪☆

Going bananas

⊙ When does a cart come before a horse?

🅰 In the dictionary!

☆✪☆✪☆✪☆✪☆

⊙ **Which English King invented the fireplace?**

🅰 **Alfred the grate!**

☆✪☆✪☆✪☆✪☆

⊙ When is a lion not a lion?

🅰 When it turns into its cage!

☆✪☆✪☆✪☆✪☆

⊙ **How do you contact a fish?**

🅰 **Drop him a line!**

☆✪☆✪☆✪☆✪☆

⊙ Why do gorillas have big noses?

🅰 Because they've got big fingers

☆✪☆✪☆✪☆✪☆

⊙ **If the red house is on the right side and the blue house is on the left, where's the white house?**

🅰 **Washington D.C.**

☆✪☆✪☆✪☆✪☆

Q Why did the cat say moo?

A It was learning a foreign language

☆✪☆✪☆✪☆✪☆

Q **What has four legs and goes "oom-oom"**

A **A cow walking backwards**

☆✪☆✪☆✪☆✪☆

Beth: Do you know why Mickey Mouse bought a telescope?

Libbe: No, why?

Beth: Because he wanted to see Pluto!

☆✪☆✪☆✪☆✪☆

Q Why did the man at the orange juice factory get the sack?

A He couldn't concentrate!

☆✪☆✪☆✪☆✪☆

Q **What do you get if you cross an elephant and a kangaroo?**

A **Big holes all over Australia!**

Techno ticklers

⊙ **Why did the gorilla log on to the Internet?**

🅐 **To check his chimpanzee-mail**

☆✪☆✪☆✪☆✪☆

⊙ When do e-mails stop being in black and white?

🅐 When they are read

☆✪☆✪☆✪☆✪☆

⊙ **How do you stop your laptop batteries from running out?**

🅐 **Hide their trainers**

☆✪☆✪☆✪☆✪☆

Helpline? I've just pushed some bacon into my disk drive!

Has your computer stopped working?

No, but there's a lot of crackling

☆✪☆✪☆✪☆✪☆

⊙ **Why didn't Vikings send e-mails?**

🅐 **They preferred using Norse code**

Mad world

What do you get if you cross a snowman with a vampire?

Frostbite

☆✪☆✪☆✪☆✪☆

Why don't bats live alone?

They like hanging out with their friends

☆✪☆✪☆✪☆✪☆

Why are ghosts such bad magicians?

You can see right through all their tricks

☆✪☆✪☆✪☆✪☆

Mother: Why did that spaceship land outside your bedroom?

Son: I must have left the landing light on.

☆✪☆✪☆✪☆✪☆

What do you give a horse with a cold?

Cough stirrup

☆✪☆✪☆✪☆✪☆

What do you get when you cross a telephone with a very big American footballer?

A wide receiver!

31

Ghoulishly funny

⊙ Why does Dracula drink blood?

🅰 Because coffee keeps him awake all day!

☆✪☆✪☆✪☆✪☆

⊙ **How do you know when there's a monster in your bath?**

🅰 **You can't get the shower curtain closed**

⊙ **Why are vampires so polite?**

🅰 **They always say "fangs"**

☆✪☆✪☆✪☆✪☆

John: Are you having a birthday party this year?

Ben: No, I'm having a witch do.

John: What's a witch do?

Ben: She flies around on a broomstick casting spells.

☆✪☆✪☆✪☆✪☆

⊙ **Which vampire tried to eat James Bond?**

🅰 **Ghould-finger**

◉ What should you do if a monster runs through your front door?

A Run through the back door

☆✪☆✪☆✪☆✪☆

◉ **What can a monster do that you can't?**

A **Count up to 30 on his fingers!**

☆✪☆✪☆✪☆✪☆

◉ What do you get if you cross a big, green monster with a fountain pen?

A The Ink-credible Hulk

☆✪☆✪☆✪☆✪☆

◉ **Why did the monster have red ears and a green nose?**

A **So he could hide in the rhubarb patch**

☆✪☆✪☆✪☆✪☆

◉ Why was the pelican asked to leave the hotel?

A Because he had a huge bill!

☆✪☆✪☆✪☆✪☆

Q Knock, knock!
Who's there?
Albert
Albert who?
turn over for answer!

turn over for answer!

Crazy as a coconut

Mother: Why are you home from school so early?

Son: I was the only one who could answer a question.

Mother: Oh, really? What was the question?

Son: Who threw the book at the headteacher?

☆✪☆✪☆✪☆✪☆

⊙ **What's big and grey and red?**

Ⓐ **A sunburnt elephant!**

A Albert you don't know who it is **!**

⊙ **Why did the cookie go to see the doctor?**

Ⓐ **Because she was feeling crumby**

☆✪☆✪☆✪☆✪☆

⊙ What do you call a multi-storey pig pen?

Ⓐ A sty-scraper

☆✪☆✪☆✪☆✪☆

⊙ **What kind of driver never gets a speeding ticket?**

Ⓐ **A screwdriver**

☆✪☆✪☆✪☆✪☆

Out of this world!

Q Where do astronauts leave their spaceships?

A At parking meteors!

☆✪☆✪☆✪☆✪☆

Q **What holds the Moon up?**

A **Moon beams!**

☆✪☆✪☆✪☆✪☆

Q What do you call an overweight E.T.?

A An extra cholesterol!

☆✪☆✪☆✪☆✪☆

Q **How do you get a baby astronaut to sleep?**

A **You rock-et!**

☆✪☆✪☆✪☆✪☆

First spaceman: I'm starving!

Second spaceman: So am I, it must be launch time!

☆✪☆✪☆✪☆✪☆

Q **How do robots shave?**

A **With laser blades**

☆✪☆✪☆✪☆✪☆

Q How do spacemen pass the time on a long mission?

A They play astronauts and crosses

☆✪☆✪☆✪☆✪☆

Pupil: I want to be an astronaut when I grow up!

Teacher: What high hopes you have!

Q **What do you call a robot that always takes the longest route round?**

A **R2-detour**

☆✪☆✪☆✪☆✪☆

Q Where do Martians go for a drink?

A To the Mars bar

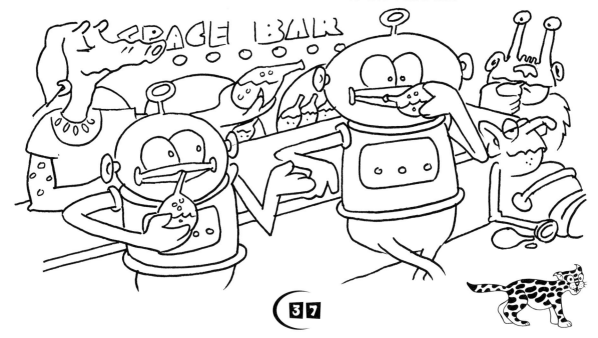

Slapstick

⊙ Why didn't the skeleton go to the dance?

🅰 He had no body to go with

☆✪☆✪☆✪☆✪☆

⊙ Why did the spider cross the road?

🅰 To get to the other web site

☆✪☆✪☆✪☆✪☆

⊙ **Why was the chicken afraid of the turkey?**

🅰 **Because it was a chicken!**

☆✪☆✪☆✪☆✪☆

⊙ What do you get from a pampered cow?

🅰 Spoiled milk

☆✪☆✪☆✪☆✪☆

A small boy was lost, so he went up to a policeman and said, "I've lost my dad!"
The policeman said, "Okay, what's he like?" to which the little boy said, "Beer and football!"

⊙ **Why did the idiot stand on his head?**

🅰 **His feet were tired**

☆✪☆✪☆✪☆✪☆

Q Why wouldn't the butterfly go to the dance?

A Because it was a moth-ball

☆✪☆✪☆✪☆✪☆

Q **Why can't a bike stand up by itself?**

A **Because it's two tired**

☆✪☆✪☆✪☆✪☆

Q Do you think it's hard to spot a leopard?

A No, they come that way!

☆✪☆✪☆✪☆✪☆

Q **What did the blanket say to the bed?**

A **I've got you covered!**

☆✪☆✪☆✪☆✪☆

Q Why are elephants so wrinkly?

A Have you ever tried to iron one?

Techno ticklers

Why couldn't the apple send an e-mail to the orange?

Because the lime was engaged

☆✪☆✪☆✪☆✪☆

Mum, Dad's broken my computer!

When did he do that?

When I dropped it on his head!

☆✪☆✪☆✪☆✪☆

Why do beavers spend so much time on the Internet?

They never want to log off

☆✪☆✪☆✪☆✪☆

Did you hear about the monkey who left bits of his dinner all over the computer?

His dad went bananas!

☆✪☆✪☆✪☆✪☆

How do werewolves sign the bottom of their e-mails?

Beast wishes

Going bananas

Q How do crazy people go through the forest?

A They go down the psycho path

☆✪☆✪☆✪☆✪☆

Q What's a haunted chicken called?

A A poultry-geist

☆✪☆✪☆✪☆✪☆

Q Why did the pony cough?

A He was a little hoarse!

☆✪☆✪☆✪☆✪☆

Q What do you call a ghost who haunts the town hall?

A A night mayor

☆✪☆✪☆✪☆✪☆

A policeman was interviewing a bank manager after the bank had been robbed by the same man three times. "Did you notice anything special about him?" asked the policeman. "Yes," replied the manager. "He was better dressed each time."

☆✪☆✪☆✪☆✪☆

Q What's a ghost's favourite food?

A I-scream!

Crazy as a coconut

◉ What's got a trunk, lots of keys and four legs?

A A piano up a tree

☆✪☆✪☆✪☆✪☆

◉ Why did the monkey cross the road?

A Because there was a banana on the other side

◉ How many ears did Davy Crockett have?

A Three – his left ear, his right ear, and his wild front ear!

☆✪☆✪☆✪☆✪☆

◉ What's grey, with big ears and a trunk?

A A mouse on holiday

Q What do you get if you cross a cow and a rabbit?

A A hare in your milk!

☆✪☆✪☆✪☆✪☆

Q When are eyes not eyes?

A When the wind makes them water

☆✪☆✪☆✪☆✪☆

Q How did the farmer mend the hole in his trousers?

A He used cabbage patches!

☆✪☆✪☆✪☆✪☆

Q What did one plate say to the other plate?

A Lunch is on me

☆✪☆✪☆✪☆✪☆

Q Why did the girl blush when she opened the fridge?

A She saw the salad dressing!

☆✪☆✪☆✪☆✪☆

Q Knock, knock!
Who's there?
Rita
Rita who?
turn over for answer!

School daze

Q Why was the headteacher worried?

A There were too many rulers in her school!

☆✪☆✪☆✪☆✪☆

Teacher: Can't you retain anything in your head overnight?

Pupil: Of course, I've had this cold in my head for two days!

☆✪☆✪☆✪☆✪☆

A Rita book, you might learn something!

Teacher: Can anyone tell me what sort of animal a slug is?

Pupil: It's a snail with a housing problem!

☆✪☆✪☆✪☆✪☆

Teacher: Would you two at the back of the room stop passing notes!

Pupil: We're not passing notes. We're playing cards!

☆✪☆✪☆✪☆✪☆

Teacher: What can we do to stop polluting our waters?

Pupil: Stop taking baths?

☆✪☆✪☆✪☆✪☆

Christmas goodies

Q Where do snowmen keep their money?

A In a snowbank!

☆✪☆✪☆✪☆✪☆

Q What do you call a penguin in the Sahara desert?

A Lost!

Q How do snowmen travel?

A By ice-icle!

☆✪☆✪☆✪☆✪☆

Q Which reindeer have the shortest legs?

A The smallest ones!

☆✪☆✪☆✪☆✪☆

Q What did the bald man say when he got a comb for Christmas?

A Thanks, I'll never part with it!

☆✪☆✪☆✪☆✪☆

Gag-tastic!

Q Where do polar bears vote?

A The North Poll

☆✪☆✪☆✪☆✪☆

Q **Why did the baker stop baking donuts?**

A **He got sick of the hole business**

Q **What streets do ghosts haunt?**

A **Dead ends!**

☆✪☆✪☆✪☆✪☆

Q How do you stop a snake from striking?

A Pay it a decent wage

Birthday bonanza!

⊙ What did the big candle say to the little candle?

A "You're too young to go out!"

☆✪☆✪☆✪☆✪☆

Bob: My birthday's coming, do you know what I need?

Hulie: Yeah, but how do you wrap a life?

☆✪☆✪☆✪☆✪☆

⊙ What do you give a full-grown gorilla for his birthday?

A Whatever he wants!

☆✪☆✪☆✪☆✪☆

⊙ **What do they serve at birthday parties in heaven?**

A **Angel cakes!**

☆✪☆✪☆✪☆✪☆

⊙ Why did the boy put candles on the toilet?

A He wanted to have a birthday potty!

☆✪☆✪☆✪☆✪☆

⊙ **How does Moby Dick celebrate his birthday?**

A **He has a whale of a time!**

Mad world

Q What's brown and sticky?

A A stick

☆✪☆✪☆✪☆✪☆

Q **Why did the parrot wear a raincoat?**

A **So he could be polyunsaturated**

☆✪☆✪☆✪☆✪☆

Q Why did the turkey cross the road?

A It was the chicken's day off

☆✪☆✪☆✪☆✪☆

Q Who was the biggest thief in history?

A Atlas, he held up the whole world!

☆✪☆✪☆✪☆✪☆

Q **What did the hat say to the scarf?**

A **You hang around while I go on ahead**

☆✪☆✪☆✪☆✪☆

Q Which is the longest word in the dictionary?

A "Smiles", because there's a mile between each "s"!

☆✪☆✪☆✪☆✪☆

Q What has four eyes but can't see?

A Mississippi

☆✪☆✪☆✪☆✪☆

Q **What do you call the elephant witch doctor?**

A **Mumbo Jumbo**

☆✪☆✪☆✪☆✪☆

Q Why does it get hot after a football game?

A Because all the fans have left!

☆✪☆✪☆✪☆✪☆

Q **Why did the shoe cry?**

A **It bit its tongue**

Q Did you hear about the man who started tap dancing?

A He broke his ankle when he fell into the sink

☆✪☆✪☆✪☆✪☆

Q **What's black and white and makes a lot of noise?**

A **A zebra with a drum kit**

Animal antics

Q What flies around your light and can bite off your head?

A A tiger moth!

☆✪☆✪☆✪☆✪☆

Q **What goes up very slowly and comes down very quickly?**

A **An elephant in a lift!**

☆✪☆✪☆✪☆✪☆

Q What is the slowest racehorse in the world?

A A clothes-horse!

☆✪☆✪☆✪☆✪☆

Q **Why did the ram fall over the cliff?**

A **He didn't see the ewe turn!**

☆✪☆✪☆✪☆✪☆

Q Why were the elephants thrown out of the swimming pool?

A Because they couldn't keep their trunks up!

☆✪☆✪☆✪☆✪☆

Q **Why are spiders like tops?**

A **They're always spinning!**

☆✪☆✪☆✪☆✪☆

Q What do you get if you cross a bumble bee and a door bell?

A A humdinger!

☆✪☆✪☆✪☆✪☆

Q Why did the dinosaur cross the road?

A Because chickens hadn't evolved yet

☆✪☆✪☆✪☆✪☆

Q Why did the cow cross the road?

A She wanted to go to the moo-vies!

☆✪☆✪☆✪☆✪☆

Q What kind of bird lays electric eggs?

A A battery hen!

☆✪☆✪☆✪☆✪☆

Q What's grey, has a wand, huge wings and gives money to elephants?

A The tusk fairy!

Going bananas

◉ When is a car not a car?

Ⓐ When it turns into a garage

☆✪☆✪☆✪☆✪☆

◉ **What did the egg say to the other egg?**

Ⓐ **Let's get cracking!**

☆✪☆✪☆✪☆✪☆

◉ What's the difference between a teacher and a train?

Ⓐ The teacher says spit your gum out and the train says "chew, chew, chew!"

☆✪☆✪☆✪☆✪☆

◉ **What is the centre of gravity?**

Ⓐ **The letter V!**

☆✪☆✪☆✪☆✪☆

◉ Why can't your nose be 12 inches long?

Ⓐ Because then it would be a foot!

Fit for fun

◉ Which goalkeeper can jump higher than a crossbar?

Ⓐ All of them, a crossbar can't jump!

☆✪☆✪☆✪☆✪☆

◉ **What kind of stories do basketball players tell?**

Ⓐ **Tall stories!**

☆✪☆✪☆✪☆✪☆

◉ How did the football pitch end up as a triangle?

Ⓐ Somebody took a corner!

☆✪☆✪☆✪☆✪☆

◉ **What do you get if you drop a piano on a team's defence?**

Ⓐ **A flat back four!**

☆✪☆✪☆✪☆✪☆

◉ What are insane Brazilian football fans called?

Ⓐ Brazil nuts!

☆✪☆✪☆✪☆✪☆

◉ **How does a scientist get their exercise?**

Ⓐ **By pumping ion!**

☆✪☆✪☆✪☆✪☆

Terrible teachers

Teacher: Fred can you find Australia on the map please?

Fred: There it is.

Teacher: Now Louise, tell me, who discovered Australia?

Louise: Fred did!

☆✪☆✪☆✪☆✪☆

Teacher: I said to draw a cow eating grass but you've only drawn the cow.

Pupil: Yes, the cow ate all the grass.

☆✪☆✪☆✪☆✪☆

Teacher: Name two pronouns.

Pupil: Who? Me?

Teacher: What kind of birds do you find in captivity?

Pupil: Jailbirds.

☆✪☆✪☆✪☆✪☆

◉   Why did the teacher wear sunglasses to lessons?

🅰   Because his class was so bright

Slapstick

Q What do you call a vampire that lives in the kitchen?

A Count Spatula

☆✪☆✪☆✪☆✪☆

Q Who serves ice cream faster than a speeding bullet?

A Scoop-erman!

☆✪☆✪☆✪☆✪☆

Q Why did the thief have a bath?

A He wanted to make a clean getaway

☆✪☆✪☆✪☆✪☆

Q Why should you take a pencil to bed?

A To draw the curtains!

☆✪☆✪☆✪☆✪☆

"Why do I have to go here?" Charlie asked when he was dropped off at the crèche at a new gym. His mother replied, "So Mummy can get skinny!" But when she picked him up 45 minutes later, he looked disappointed. "Aww, Mum," he cried. "It didn't work!"

☆✪☆✪☆✪☆✪☆

Q What do you give a sick pig?

A Oinkment

Good girls

Q What kind of girl does a mummy take on a date?

A Any old girl he can dig up

☆✪☆✪☆✪☆✪☆

Q **What do you call a girl with a frog on her head?**

A **Lily!**

☆✪☆✪☆✪☆✪☆

Q What did the skeleton say to his girlfriend?

A I love every bone in your body

☆✪☆✪☆✪☆✪☆

My girlfriend talks so much that when we go on holiday, I have to spread suntan lotion on her tongue

☆✪☆✪☆✪☆✪☆

Q Why did the wizard turn the girl into a mouse?

A Because she ratted on him

☆✪☆✪☆✪☆✪☆

School Doctor: I'm afraid your daughter needs glasses.

Parent: How can you tell?

School Doctor: By the way she came in through the window.

Mother: Did you get a good place in the geography test?

Daughter: Yes, I sat next to the cleverest kid in the class.

☆✪☆✪☆✪☆✪☆

Rich: My girlfriend says that if I don't give up golf she'll leave me

Karl: That's really tough!

Rich: Yeah, I'm going to miss her.

☆✪☆✪☆✪☆✪☆

◉ How did the witch doctor ask a girl to dance?

🅐 "Voodoo like to dance with me?"

☆✪☆✪☆✪☆✪☆

Mum: Jenny, how can you practice your trumpet and listen to the radio at the same time?

Jenny: I've got two ears.

☆✪☆✪☆✪☆✪☆

First monster: That girl over there just rolled her eyes at me.

Second monster: Well you'd better roll them back to her, she might need them.

Crazy as a coconut

○ What's brown, has a hump, and lives at the North Pole?

🅰 A lost camel

☆✪☆✪☆✪☆✪☆

○ **Why couldn't Noah play cards on the ark?**

🅰 **The elephant was standing on the deck**

○ Have you heard the joke about the garbage truck?

🅰 Don't worry, it's a load of rubbish

☆✪☆✪☆✪☆✪☆

○ What do you get when you cross an archer with a gift-wrapper?

🅰 Ribbon Hood

☆✪☆✪☆✪☆✪☆

○ **What did the policeman say to his stomach?**

🅰 **"You're under a vest!"**

☆✪☆✪☆✪☆✪☆

◉ Where do vampires keep their savings?

Ⓐ In the blood bank

☆✪☆✪☆✪☆✪☆

◉ **Why did the king go to the dentist?**

Ⓐ **He wanted to get his teeth crowned**

☆✪☆✪☆✪☆✪☆

◉ What happens to cows during an earthquake?

Ⓐ They give milk shakes!

☆✪☆✪☆✪☆✪☆

◉ **Why did the boy go out with a prune?**

Ⓐ **Because he couldn't get a date!**

☆✪☆✪☆✪☆✪☆

◉ What do you give a dog with a fever?

Ⓐ Mustard, its the best thing for a hot dog!

☆✪☆✪☆✪☆✪☆

Q Knock, knock!
Who's there?
Boo
Boo who?
turn over for answer!

Bonkers!

⊙ What's red, and flies and wobbles at the same time?

🅐 A jelly-copter

☆✪☆✪☆✪☆✪☆

⊙ **Why did the cowboy die with his boots on?**

🅐 **Because he thought it might hurt when he kicked the bucket**

☆✪☆✪☆✪☆✪☆

⊙ **Who's the biggest gangster in the sea?**

🅐 **Al Ca-prawn**

☆✪☆✪☆✪☆✪☆

⊙ How do you stop a cold getting to your chest?

🅐 Tie a knot in your neck

☆✪☆✪☆✪☆✪☆

⊙ **What's hairy and coughs?**

🅐 **A coconut with a cold**

☆✪☆✪☆✪☆✪☆

A Don't cry, it's only a joke!

Mad world

Q What's a snake's favourite subject at school?

A Hisss-tory

☆✪☆✪☆✪☆✪☆

Q **What did the duck say when she bought some lipstick?**

A **Put it on my bill**

Q **How do you stop a rhino from charging?**

A **Take away his credit card**

☆✪☆✪☆✪☆✪☆

Q What keeps musicians on Earth?

A Groov-ity

☆✪☆✪☆✪☆✪☆

Q **What did the snail say when he rode on the turtle's back?**

A **WHEEEEEEEE!!**

☆✪☆✪☆✪☆✪☆

Gag-tastic!

⊙ **What did the postcard say to the stamp?**

🅰 **Stick with me kid, and we'll go places**

☆✪☆✪☆✪☆✪☆

⊙ Why do golfers wear two pairs of trousers?

🅰 In case they get a hole in one

☆✪☆✪☆✪☆✪☆

⊙ **What's a ghost's favourite airline?**

🅰 **British Scare-ways**

☆✪☆✪☆✪☆✪☆

⊙ Why do cows use the doorbell?

🅰 Because their horns don't work!

☆✪☆✪☆✪☆✪☆

⊙ **What do you get when you cross a cow and a duck?**

🅰 **Milk and quackers**

☆✪☆✪☆✪☆✪☆

⊙ What did the grape do when it got stepped on?

🅰 It let out a little wine

☆✪☆✪☆✪☆✪☆

63

Animal antics

- **What happened when the lion ate the comedian?**

- **He felt funny!**

☆✪☆✪☆✪☆✪☆

- How long do chickens work?

- Around the cluck!

☆✪☆✪☆✪☆✪☆

- **What's grey and lights up?**

- **An electric elephant!**

☆✪☆✪☆✪☆✪☆

- What does a spider do when he gets angry?

- He goes up the wall!

☆✪☆✪☆✪☆✪☆

- **What do cows like to dance to?**

- **All types of moo-sic**

Doctor, Doctor

Doctor, Doctor, some days I feel like a tee-pee and other days I feel like a wig-wam.

You're too tents

☆✪☆✪☆✪☆✪☆

Doctor, Doctor, my eye hurts when I drink coffee

Have you tried taking the spoon out?

☆✪☆✪☆✪☆✪☆

Doctor, Doctor, I've swallowed a bone

Are you choking?

No, I really did!

☆✪☆✪☆✪☆✪☆

Doctor, Doctor, I've had tummy ache since I ate three crabs yesterday.

Did they smell bad when you took them out of their shells?

What do you mean "took them out of their shells"!

☆✪☆✪☆✪☆✪☆

Doctor, Doctor I snore so loudly I keep myself awake

Sleep in another room then

☆✪☆✪☆✪☆✪☆

Doctor, Doctor, what did the x-ray of my head show?

Absolutely nothing!

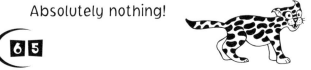

Christmas goodies

Q **What do chimps sing at Christmas?**

A **Jungle Bells, Jungle bells..!**

☆✪☆✪☆✪☆✪☆

Q How do you make a slow reindeer fast?

A Don't feed it!

☆✪☆✪☆✪☆✪☆

Q **What did the snowman order at the burger bar?**

A **Iceberg-ers with chilli sauce**

☆✪☆✪☆✪☆✪☆

Q How do you know when there's a snowman in your bed?

A You wake up wet!

☆✪☆✪☆✪☆✪☆

Q **Why did the reindeer wear sunglasses to the beach?**

A **He didn't want to be recognised!**

Going bananas

What lies on the ground, 100 feet in the air?

A dead centipede

☆✪☆✪☆✪☆✪☆

Two pieces of string met in the park one day and while one went on the slide the other went on the swings. They were having a great time until one string decided to go on the roundabout. After a while, the string felt dizzy and fell off, scraping across the ground, making a mess of one end and falling in a heap. The second string looked at him and sighed, "You're not very good on that roundabout are you?"
The first string looked at himself and said, "I'm a frayed knot."

☆✪☆✪☆✪☆✪☆

What's big and grey with horns?

An elephant marching band

☆✪☆✪☆✪☆✪☆

What sort of star is dangerous?

A shooting star!

☆✪☆✪☆✪☆✪☆

How do pigs get to the hospital?

In a ham-bulance

☆✪☆✪☆✪☆✪☆

Crazy as a coconut

Q **If you drop a white hat into the Red Sea, what does it become?**

A **Wet**

☆✪☆✪☆✪☆✪☆

Q What do whales eat?

A Fish and ships

☆✪☆✪☆✪☆✪☆

Q **What kind of mistakes do ghosts make?**

A **Boo boos**

☆✪☆✪☆✪☆✪☆

Q What did the Atlantic Ocean say to the Indian Ocean?

A Nothing, it just waved

☆✪☆✪☆✪☆✪☆

Q **How do you know when there's an elephant under your bed?**

A **Your nose touches the ceiling**

School daze

What's black and white all over and difficult?

An exam paper!

☆✪☆✪☆✪☆✪☆

Teacher: Neil, you missed school yesterday, didn't you?

Neil: Not a bit!

☆✪☆✪☆✪☆✪☆

Teacher: What is the most common phrase used in school?

Pupil: I don't know.

Teacher: Correct!

☆✪☆✪☆✪☆✪☆

Teacher: Do you file your nails, Billy?

Billy: No, I just throw them away!

☆✪☆✪☆✪☆

Mother: Let me see your report, Danny.

Danny: Here it is Mum, but don't show it to Dad. He's been helping me!

☆✪☆✪☆✪☆

Teacher: What is a comet?

Pupil: A star with a tail.

Teacher: Can you name one?

Pupil: Lassie!

Slapstick

Q Why did the chewing gum cross the road?

A It was stuck to the chicken's foot!

☆✪☆✪☆✪☆✪☆

Q When is it bad luck to be followed by a black cat?

A When you're a mouse!

☆✪☆✪☆✪☆✪☆

Q Why couldn't Cinderella get on the football team?

A Because she ran away from the ball

☆✪☆✪☆✪☆✪☆

Q Where do bees go to the toilet?

A At the BP station!

☆✪☆✪☆✪☆✪☆

Q What happens if you eat yeast and shoe polish?

A Every morning you'll rise and shine!

☆✪☆✪☆✪☆✪☆

Q What runs around a farm but never moves?

A A fence

☆✪☆✪☆✪☆✪☆

Q What makes a chess player happy?

A Taking a knight off

☆✪☆✪☆✪☆✪☆

Q **What do rabbits use to keep their fur tidy?**

A **Hare-spray**

☆✪☆✪☆✪☆✪☆

Q Where do monsters go on holiday?

A The Isle of Fright!

☆✪☆✪☆✪☆✪☆

Q **What do you get if Batman and Robin get crushed by a steam roller?**

A **Flatman and ribbon**

☆✪☆✪☆✪☆✪☆

Q What would you find on a haunted beach?

A A sand witch

Bad boys

Why did the boy take an aspirin after hearing a werewolf howl?

A Because it gave him an eerie ache

☆✪☆✪☆✪☆✪☆

Brad: My brother's just opened a shop.

Kevin: Really? How's he doing?

Brad: Six months. He opened it with a crowbar!

☆✪☆✪☆✪☆✪☆

My brother's looking for a girlfriend. The trouble is, he can't find a girl who loves him as much as he loves himself.

☆✪☆✪☆✪☆✪☆

Little Brother: I'm buying a sea horse.

Big Brother: Why?

Little Brother: Because I want to play water polo!

☆✪☆✪☆✪☆✪☆

Ned: Does your brother keep himself clean?

Jim: Oh, yes! He takes a bath every month whether he needs one or not.

☆✪☆✪☆✪☆✪☆

Peter: My brother wants to work really badly!

Anita: As I remember, he usually does!

Q What's the difference between a crossword expert, a greedy boy and a pot of glue?

A A crossword expert is a good puzzler and the greedy boy's a pud guzzler!
The pot of glue? Oh, that's where you get stuck!

☆✪☆✪☆✪☆✪☆

Tony: Why is your brother always flying off the handle?

Guy: Because he's got a screw loose!

☆✪☆✪☆✪☆✪☆

Q Why did the boy take a clock and a bird out for Halloween?

A It was for 'tick or tweet'!

One day Sam was walking down the street when he saw a sea monster standing on the corner looking lost. Sam put a lead on the sea monster and took him to the police station.
"You should take him to the museum," said the policeman.
The next day the policeman saw Sam in the town again with the monster on the lead.
"I told you to take him to the museum," said the policeman.
"I did," said Sam, "and today I'm taking him to the cinema!"

Gag-tastic!

◉ **What did the judge say when the skunk walked in the court room?**

🅰 **"Odour in the court!"**

☆✪☆✪☆✪☆✪☆

◉ What happens if a big, hairy monster sits in front of you at the cinema?

🅰 You miss most of the film!

☆✪☆✪☆✪☆✪☆

◉ **What sort of pie can fly?**

🅰 **A magpie**

☆✪☆✪☆✪☆✪☆

◉ Why did the boy put sugar on his pillow before going to sleep?

🅰 So he could have sweet dreams

☆✪☆✪☆✪☆✪☆

◉ **What has four wheels and flies?**

🅰 **A rubbish truck!**

Ghoulishly funny

Why do mummies make great spies?

They're good at keeping things under wraps

☆✪☆✪☆✪☆✪☆

Why don't skeletons like spicy food?

They can't stomach it!

☆✪☆✪☆✪☆✪☆

What has a green spotted body, twelve hairy legs and big eyes on stalks?

I don't know but there's one crawling up your leg!

What's a vampire's favourite sport?

Bat-minton

☆✪☆✪☆✪☆✪☆

What kind of monster can sit on the end of your finger?

The bogeyman

☆✪☆✪☆✪☆✪☆

What did the monster eat after the dentist pulled his tooth out?

The dentist!

☆✪☆✪☆✪☆✪☆

Going bananas

◉ What did the fish say when it swam into the wall?

🅐 Dam!

☆✪☆✪☆✪☆✪☆

◉ **Which weighs more, a ton of feathers or a ton of bricks?**

🅐 **Neither; they both weigh a ton!**

☆✪☆✪☆✪☆✪☆

◉ Which cats love the water?

🅐 Octo-Pussies

☆✪☆✪☆✪☆✪☆

◉ **What do you call a sleeping bull?**

🅐 **A bulldozer**

☆✪☆✪☆✪☆✪☆

◉ What only works when it's fired?

🅐 A rocket

☆✪☆✪☆✪☆✪☆

◉ **How do you catch a squirrel?**

🅐 **Climb up a tree and act like a nut!**

☆✪☆✪☆✪☆✪☆

Q What goes up and down but doesn't move?

A The temperature!

☆✪☆✪☆✪☆✪☆

Q **What's a hedgehog's favourite food?**

A **Prickled onions**

☆✪☆✪☆✪☆✪☆

Q What kind of car does Luke Skywalker drive?

A A Toy-yoda

☆✪☆✪☆✪☆✪☆

Q **What stories do the ship captain's children like to hear?**

A **Ferry tales**

☆✪☆✪☆✪☆✪☆

Q What do you get if you cross a sheep and a porcupine?

A An animal that knits its own jumpers

Animal antics

⊙ On which day do lions eat most people?

🅰 Chews-day!

☆✪☆✪☆✪☆✪☆

⊙ **Why did the chicken cross the road?**

🅰 **To get to the other side**

☆✪☆✪☆✪☆✪☆

⊙ Why did the fly fly?

🅰 Because the spider spied 'er!

☆✪☆✪☆✪☆✪☆

⊙ **What happened to the leopard who took three baths a day?**

🅰 **After a week he was spotless!**

☆✪☆✪☆✪☆✪☆

⊙ What do you call a rooster who wakes you up at the same time every morning?

🅰 An alarm cluck!

☆✪☆✪☆✪☆✪☆

⊙ **What's grey and wrinkly and jumps every twenty seconds?**

🅰 **An elephant with hiccups!**

☆✪☆✪☆✪☆✪☆

Q What do you get if you sit under a cow?

A A pat on the head!

☆✪☆✪☆✪☆✪☆

Q What happens when geese land in a volcano?

A They cook their own gooses!

☆✪☆✪☆✪☆✪☆

Q What do you get if you cross a tiger and a sheep?

A A stripy sweater!

☆✪☆✪☆✪☆✪☆

Q Which animal always goes to bed with its shoes on?

A A horse!

☆✪☆✪☆✪☆✪☆

Q How does an elephant get down from a tree?

A He sits on a leaf and waits till autumn!

Mad world

⊙ How do you make a tissue dance?

🄰 Put a little boogey in it!

☆✪☆✪☆✪☆✪☆

⊙ **Why is it a bad idea to write a letter on an empty stomach?**

🄰 **Because it's much better to write on paper**

⊙ **Why don't skeletons fight?**

🄰 **They haven't got the guts**

☆✪☆✪☆✪☆✪☆

⊙ Who speaks on behalf of the Ghosts Union?

🄰 Their Spooks-person

☆✪☆✪☆✪☆✪☆

⊙ **Which month do soldiers hate most?**

🄰 **March!**

☆✪☆✪☆✪☆✪☆

Why did the boy study in the aeroplane?

He wanted a higher education

☆✪☆✪☆✪☆✪☆

A sloth was out for a walk when he was mugged by four snails. After recovering his wits, he went to make a police report. "Can you describe the snails?" asked the officer. "Not really," said the sloth "it all happened so fast!"

☆✪☆✪☆✪☆✪☆

Why do elephants wear sneakers?

So they can creep up on mice!

☆✪☆✪☆✪☆✪☆

What do dogs eat at the cinema?

Pup-corn

☆✪☆✪☆✪☆✪☆

What do you get if you cross a shark and a parrot?

An animal that talks your head off

☆✪☆✪☆✪☆✪☆

Q **Knock, knock!**
Who's there?
Lettuce
Lettuce who?
turn over for answer!

Doctor, Doctor

Doctor: I think you're crazy!

Patient: I want a second opinion.

Doctor: OK, you also smell terrible!

☆✪☆✪☆✪☆✪☆

Doctor, Doctor, I keep thinking I'm invisible

Who said that?

☆✪☆✪☆✪☆✪☆

Tell me straight Doc, Is it bad?

Well, I wouldn't start watching any new soap operas!

☆✪☆✪☆✪☆✪☆

Doctor, Doctor, I feel like a needle

I see your point!

☆✪☆✪☆✪☆✪☆

Doctor, Doctor, I've got a split personality

Well both of you had better sit down then!

☆✪☆✪☆✪☆✪☆

A Lettuce in, it's cold outside!

School daze

Teacher: If you had seven apples on your desk and the boy next to you took four what would you have?

Pupil: A fight!

☆✪☆✪☆✪☆✪☆

Teacher: Billie, stop daydreaming.

Billie: I wasn't daydreaming, I was having a nap!

Teacher: Were you copying his sums?

Pupil: No Sir, just seeing if he got mine right!

☆✪☆✪☆✪☆✪☆

Teacher: This note from your father looks like your handwriting!

Pupil: Well, he did borrow my pen!

☆✪☆✪☆✪☆✪☆

Teacher: Sam, put some more water in the fish tank.

Pupil: I put some in last week and they haven't drunk that yet!

Crazy as a coconut

Q What do you say to a cow that crosses in front of your car?

A Mooo-ve over!

☆✪☆✪☆✪☆✪☆

Q **What do ducks watch on TV?**

A **Duck-umentaries**

☆✪☆✪☆✪☆✪☆

Q Why did the bird go to hospital?

A To get tweet-ment

☆✪☆✪☆✪☆✪☆

Q **What two days of the week start with the letter "T"?**

A **Today and Tomorrow!**

☆✪☆✪☆✪☆✪☆

Q Why didn't the flower ride his bike?

A Because he had lost his petals!

☆✪☆✪☆✪☆✪☆

Q **Why do dragons sleep during the day?**

A **So they can fight knights**

☆✪☆✪☆✪☆✪☆

Q What kind of ghosts do they have in hospital?

A Surgical spirits

☆✪☆✪☆✪☆✪☆

Q What do you call artificial spaghetti?

A Mock-aroni!

Q What were the only creatures not to go into the Ark in pairs?

A The maggots, they went in an apple

☆✪☆✪☆✪☆✪☆

Q Why is basketball such a messy sport?

A Because the players dribble all over the floor!

Techno ticklers

⊙ **Why was the computer in pain?**

Ⓐ **It had a slipped disk!**

☆✪☆✪☆✪☆✪☆

Brian: I've lost my dog!

Kate: Have you tried putting a message on the Internet?

Brian: Don't be silly, my dog never reads e-mails!

☆✪☆✪☆✪☆✪☆

⊙ **Why did the farmer hang raincoats in his orchard?**

Ⓐ **Someone told him he should get an apple Mac**

Teacher: Shall I put the school computer on?

Pupil: No Miss, the dress you're wearing looks fine.

☆✪☆✪☆✪☆✪☆

⊙ **Why was the skeleton using the Internet?**

Ⓐ **To bone up on his schoolwork**

Slapstick

Q Why can't you play tricks on snakes?

A Because you can't pull their legs

☆✪☆✪☆✪☆✪☆

Q What runs but can't walk?

A A tap!

☆✪☆✪☆✪☆✪☆

Q Why would Snow White make a great judge?

A Because she's the fairest in the land

☆✪☆✪☆✪☆✪☆

Q How does a witch tell the time?

A She looks at her witch watch

☆✪☆✪☆✪☆✪☆

Q Where did the king keep his armies?

A Up his sleevies

☆✪☆✪☆✪☆✪☆

Q What kind of cats like going bowling?

A Alley cats

☆✪☆✪☆✪☆✪☆

Animal antics

Q **Why is the desert lion so popular at Christmas?**

A **Because he has sandy claws!**

☆✪☆✪☆✪☆✪☆

Q Why did the elephant paint himself in different colours?

A Because he wanted to hide in the colouring box

☆✪☆✪☆✪☆✪☆

Q **What kind of doctors are like spiders?**

A **Spin doctors**

☆✪☆✪☆✪☆✪☆

Q What do you call a pig with no clothes on?

A Streaky bacon!

☆✪☆✪☆✪☆✪☆

Q **What do you get if you cross a chicken with a cement mixer?**

A **A brick-layer!**

Fit for fun

⦿ **Why did the footballer hold his boot to his ear?**

Ⓐ **Because he liked sole music!**

☆✪☆✪☆✪☆✪☆

⦿ Why don't fish play tennis?

Ⓐ They don't like getting close to the net

☆✪☆✪☆✪☆✪☆

⦿ **What lights up a stadium?**

Ⓐ **A football match!**

☆✪☆✪☆✪☆✪☆

⦿ Why did the goal post get angry?

Ⓐ Because the bar was rattled!

☆✪☆✪☆✪☆✪☆

⦿ **If you have a referee in football and an umpire in cricket, what do you have in bowls?**

Ⓐ **Cornflakes!**

☆✪☆✪☆✪☆✪☆

⦿ Why do marathon runners make such good students?

Ⓐ Because education pays off in the long run!

Going bananas

Q What's the best day to go to the beach?

A Sunday, of course!

☆✪☆✪☆✪☆✪☆

Q How do you make a bandstand?

A Take away their chairs!

Teacher: Michael, I told you to write this poem out ten times to improve your handwriting and you've only done it seven times.

Michael: Looks like my counting isn't very good either!

☆✪☆✪☆✪☆✪☆

Bonkers!

Q How do you make milk shake?

A Give it a good scare

☆✪☆✪☆✪☆✪☆

Q Why isn't it safe to sleep on trains?

A Because they run over sleepers

☆✪☆✪☆✪☆✪☆

Anne: In the park this morning I was surrounded by lions!

Debbie: Lions! In the park?

Anne: Well, dandelions!

☆✪☆✪☆✪☆✪☆

Q How do you cure a headache?

A Put your head through a window and the pane will disappear

☆✪☆✪☆✪☆✪☆

Customer: I want a hair cut please.

Barber: Certainly, which one?

☆✪☆✪☆✪☆✪☆

Q Did you hear about the scientist who put dynamite in his fridge?

A It blew his cool

☆✪☆✪☆✪☆✪☆

Gag-tastic!

Q Why did the farmer buy a brown cow?

A Because he wanted chocolate milk

☆✪☆✪☆✪☆✪☆

Q What has one horn and gives milk

A A milk float

☆✪☆✪☆✪☆✪☆

Q What did the baby light bulb say to it's mum?

A I love you watts and watts!

☆✪☆✪☆✪☆✪☆

Q What did one star say to the other star when they met?

A "Glad to meteor!"

☆✪☆✪☆✪☆✪☆

Craig: I tried to send an e-mail but I broke my computer.

Phil: How did you do that?

Craig: I think it was when I tried pushing it through the letterbox!

☆✪☆✪☆✪☆✪☆

Q What tools do you need in maths class?

A Multi-pliers

⊙ What kind of key opens a banana?

🅰 A mon-key!

☆✪☆✪☆✪☆✪☆

⊙ **Why do birds watch the news?**

🅰 **To get the feather forecast**

☆✪☆✪☆✪☆✪☆

⊙ Why did the dog cross the road?

🅰 To get to the barking lot

☆✪☆✪☆✪☆✪☆

⊙ **What do baby ghosts drink?**

🅰 **Evaporated milk**

⊙ **Why are giraffes so slow to apologize?**

🅰 **It takes them a long time to swallow their pride**

☆✪☆✪☆✪☆✪☆

⊙ What do you call a surgeon with eight arms?

🅰 A doct-opus!

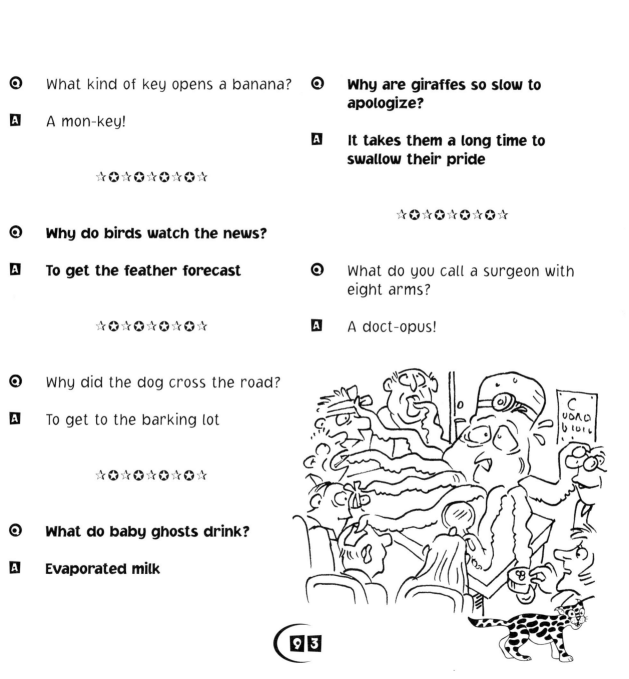

What do you call...

⊙ **What do you call a man with a spade on his head?**

🅐 **Doug**

☆✪☆✪☆✪☆✪☆

⊙ What do you call a man without a spade on his head?

🅐 Douglas

☆✪☆✪☆✪☆✪☆

⊙ **What do you call a woman with a twig on her head?**

🅐 **Hazel**

☆✪☆✪☆✪☆✪☆

⊙ What do you call a man with a mat on his head?

🅐 Neil

☆✪☆✪☆✪☆✪☆

⊙ **What do you call a woman with a cat on her head?**

🅐 **Kitty**

Ghoulishly funny

◉ **Why doesn't Dracula have many friends?**

🅰 **Because he's a pain in the neck!**

☆✪☆✪☆✪☆✪☆

◉ What did the Mummy ghost say to the baby ghost?

🅰 "Don't spook unless your spooken to!"

☆✪☆✪☆✪☆✪☆

◉ **Why was the monster standing on his head?**

🅰 **He was turning things over in his mind**

☆✪☆✪☆✪☆✪☆

◉ Why do witches think they're funny?

🅰 Every time they look in the mirror, it cracks up

☆✪☆✪☆✪☆✪☆

◉ **What do monsters order at the burger bar?**

🅰 **Hand-burgers**

☆✪☆✪☆✪☆✪☆

◉ What happened when the two monsters had a race?

🅰 One ran in short bursts, the other ran in burst shorts

Crazy as a coconut

Q Why do elephants never forget?

A Because nobody ever tells them anything

☆✪☆✪☆✪☆✪☆

Q What do you call a fairy who doesn't bath?

A Stinkerbell!

Three year old Timmy had fine, fly-away hair, so his mother often wet it to comb it into place. One morning as she applied water and slicked his hair back, she announced it was time for him to get another haircut. "Mum," Timmy replied, "if you didn't water it so much, it wouldn't grow so fast!"

☆✪☆✪☆✪☆✪☆

Q Why are fish so clever?

A Because they live in schools

☆✪☆✪☆✪☆✪☆

Q Why is six scared of seven?

A Because 7-8-9!

Fit for fun

⊙ What part of a football pitch smells the nicest?

🅰 The scent-er spot!

☆✪☆✪☆✪☆✪☆

⊙ **How do you stop squirrels playing cricket in the garden?**

🅰 **Hide the ball, it drives them nuts!**

☆✪☆✪☆✪☆✪☆

⊙ What is a runner's favourite subject in school?

🅰 Jog-raphy!

☆✪☆✪☆✪☆✪☆

Manager: I'll give you £50 a week to start with and £100 a week in a year's time?

Young player: OK, I'll come back in a year's time.

☆✪☆✪☆✪☆✪☆

⊙ Why didn't the dog want to play tennis?

🅰 Because it was a boxer!

☆✪☆✪☆✪☆✪☆

⊙ **What should a football team do if the pitch is flooded?**

🅰 **Bring on their subs!**

Mad world

◉ What type of bow can't be tied?

🅐 A rainbow

☆✪☆✪☆✪☆✪☆

◉ **Did you hear about the wooden car with the wooden wheels and the wooden engine?**

🅐 **It wooden go!**

☆✪☆✪☆✪☆✪☆

◉ What did the teddy bear say when he was offered dessert?

🅐 No thanks, I'm stuffed!

☆✪☆✪☆✪☆✪☆

◉ **Which letters aren't in the alphabet?**

🅐 **The ones in the post!**

☆✪☆✪☆✪☆✪☆

◉ Where do computers go to dance?

🅐 To the disc-o

☆✪☆✪☆✪☆✪☆

◉ **When does it rain money?**

🅐 **When there's a change in the weather**

☆✪☆✪☆✪☆✪☆

Q Where do bulls get their messages?

A On a bull-etin board

☆✪☆✪☆✪☆✪☆

Q When do ghosts usually appear?

A Just before someone screams

Q Why is the letter "G" scary?

A It turns a host into a ghost

☆✪☆✪☆✪☆✪☆

Q Why do bagpipers walk while they play?

A To get away from the noise!

Doctor, Doctor

Doctor, Doctor, my son has swallowed my pen, what should I do?

Use a pencil until I get there

☆✪☆✪☆✪☆✪☆

Doctor, Doctor, you have to help me out!

Certainly, which way did you come in?

☆✪☆✪☆✪☆✪☆

Doctor, Doctor, I think I'm a dog

How long have you felt like this?

Ever since I was a puppy!

☆✪☆✪☆✪☆✪☆

Doctor, Doctor, I feel like a pack of cards

I'll deal with you later!

☆✪☆✪☆✪☆✪☆

Doctor, Doctor, I feel like a burglar!

Have you taken anything for it?

Slapstick

⊙ What has one head, one foot and four legs?

🅰 A bed

☆✪☆✪☆✪☆✪☆

⊙ **Why did the teacher jump into the lake?**

🅰 **Because she wanted to test the water!**

☆✪☆✪☆✪☆✪☆

⊙ What should you say when you meet a ghost?

🅰 "How do you boo?"

☆✪☆✪☆✪☆✪☆

⊙ **What goes through towns, up and over hills, but doesn't move?**

🅰 **The road!**

☆✪☆✪☆✪☆✪☆

⊙ What do you call a gorilla with a banana in each ear?

🅰 Anything you like, he can't hear you!

☆✪☆✪☆✪☆✪☆

⊙ **When is the vet busiest?**

🅰 **When it's raining cats and dogs**

☆✪☆✪☆✪☆✪☆

Animal antics

⊙ **What does the lion say to his friends before they go hunting?**

Ⓐ **"Let us prey!"**

☆✪☆✪☆✪☆✪☆

⊙ When does a ghost need a license?

Ⓐ During the "haunting" season

☆✪☆✪☆✪☆✪☆

⊙ **Why does a rooster watch TV?**

Ⓐ **For hen-tertainment!**

☆✪☆✪☆✪☆✪☆

⊙ Why did the chicken cross the "net"?

Ⓐ It wanted to get to the other site!

☆✪☆✪☆✪☆✪☆

⊙ **What has three tails, four trunks and six feet?**

Ⓐ **An elephant with spare parts!**

What do you call...

- **What do you call a man with a truck on his head?**

- **Laurie**

☆✪☆✪☆✪☆✪☆

- What do you call a woman with a breeze on her head?

- Gail

☆✪☆✪☆✪☆✪☆

- What do you call a woman with slates on her head?

- Ruth

☆✪☆✪☆✪☆✪☆

- **What do you call a man with turf on his head?**

- **Pete**

☆✪☆✪☆✪☆✪☆

- What do you call a girl with a tennis racket on her head?

- Annette

☆✪☆✪☆✪☆✪☆

Q Knock, knock!
Who's there?
Howl
Howl who?
turn over for answer!

Gag-tastic!

Q Were you long in the hospital?

A No, I was the same size that I am now

☆✪☆✪☆✪☆✪☆

Q **What do you call a bear with no socks on?**

A **Bare-foot**

☆✪☆✪☆✪☆✪☆

Q **How do hedgehogs play leapfrog?**

A **Very carefully!**

☆✪☆✪☆✪☆✪☆

One day three-year-old Gail and her mum were out shopping. Everything the mum said or did, Gail asked, "Why?" Finally, mum said, "Gail, please stop asking me why." After a short silence, she looked at her and asked, "Okay, how come?"

☆✪☆✪☆✪☆✪☆

Q **Why was the maths book sad?**

A **Because it had so many problems**

☆✪☆✪☆✪☆✪☆

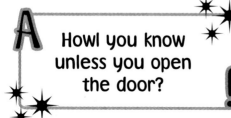

A Howl you know unless you open the door?

Birthday bonanza

Karl: When's your birthday?

Mark: November 13.

Karl: What year?

Mark: Every year!

☆✪☆✪☆✪☆✪☆

◉ What has wings, a long tail and wears a bow?

🅰 A birthday pheasant!

☆✪☆✪☆✪☆✪☆

◉ **What song should you sing to a wildebeest on his birthday?**

🅰 **"Happy Birthday To Gnu!"**

"Doctor, I get heartburn every time I eat birthday cake!"

"Try taking off the candles first!"

☆✪☆✪☆✪☆✪☆

◉ **What did the hungry monster get after he'd eaten too much ice cream?**

🅰 **More ice cream!**

Going bananas

⊙ **Why did the jelly wobble?**

🅰 **Because it saw the milk shake!**

☆✪☆✪☆✪☆✪☆

⊙ What did the frog order at the burger bar?

🅰 French flies and a diet croak

☆✪☆✪☆✪☆✪☆

⊙ **Which pet makes the loudest noise?**

🅰 **A trum-pet!**

☆✪☆✪☆✪☆✪☆

⊙ Why is turtle wax so expensive?

🅰 Because turtles have such tiny ears

☆✪☆✪☆✪☆✪☆

⊙ **Why did the boy throw a glass of water out the window?**

🅰 **He wanted to see a waterfall**

☆✪☆✪☆✪☆✪☆

⊙ What do cats eat for breakfast?

🅰 Mice crispies!

☆✪☆✪☆✪☆✪☆

Terrible teachers

Teacher: Can anyone tell me how many seconds there are in a year?

Pupil: 12 – 2nd January, 2nd February...

✮✪✮✪✮✪✮✪✮

Teacher: In 1940, what were the Poles doing in Russia?

Pupil: Holding up the telegraph lines.

✮✪✮✪✮✪✮✪✮

Teacher: I wish you would pay a little attention!

Pupil: I'm paying as little as I can

✮✪✮✪✮✪✮✪✮

Teacher: How can you prove the world is round?

Pupil: I didn't say it was.

✮✪✮✪✮✪✮✪✮

Teacher: Can anyone give me the name of a liquid that won't freeze?

Pupil: Hot water.

Crazy as a coconut

Q What book tells you all about chickens?

A A hen-cyclopedia

☆✪☆✪☆✪☆✪☆

Q **What can you serve but can't eat?**

A **A tennis ball**

☆✪☆✪☆✪☆✪☆

Q What do you call a mouse that can pick up a monster?

A Sir!

☆✪☆✪☆✪☆✪☆

Q **What happened when 100 hares got loose in the centre of town?**

A **The police had to comb the area**

☆✪☆✪☆✪☆✪☆

Q What kind of building is the tallest in the world?

A A library; it has the most stories

☆✪☆✪☆✪☆✪☆

Q **Why didn't the crab share his toys?**

A **He was shellfish!**

☆✪☆✪☆✪☆✪☆

Slapstick

⊙ **Why is it hard to have a conversation with a goat?**

🅰 **Because they're always butting in**

☆✪☆✪☆✪☆✪☆

⊙ How do you prevent a summer cold?

🅰 Catch it in the winter

☆✪☆✪☆✪☆✪☆

⊙ **What two things aren't eaten for breakfast?**

🅰 **Lunch and dinner**

☆✪☆✪☆✪☆✪☆

Doctor, Doctor, I feel like an apple

We must get to the core of this problem!

☆✪☆✪☆✪☆✪☆

⊙ **What did the dirt say when it started to rain?**

🅰 **If this keeps up, my name is gonna be mud!**

☆✪☆✪☆✪☆✪☆

⊙ What's big, grey and flies straight up?

🅰 An ele-copter

☆✪☆✪☆✪☆✪☆

" So, what do you think about
this mad cow disease? "

" What do I care.
I'm a helicopter! "

Bonkers!

⊙ **Why did the clock get sick?**

A **It was run down**

✩✪✩✪✩✪✩✪✩

⊙ What smells of fish and goes round and round at 100 miles an hour?

A A goldfish in a blender

✩✪✩✪✩✪✩✪✩

Have you ever seen a man-eating tiger?

No, but in the cafe next door I once saw a man eating some chicken!

✩✪✩✪✩✪✩✪✩

Dad, there's a man at the door collecting for the new swimming pool

Give him a glass of water!

✩✪✩✪✩✪✩✪✩

⊙ **Why did the idiot have his sundial floodlit?**

A **So he could tell the time at night**

Christmas goodies

Q **What does Frosty the snowman have for breakfast?**

A **Snowflakes!**

☆✪☆✪☆✪☆✪☆

Q Where do you find reindeer?

A It depends where you left them

☆✪☆✪☆✪☆✪☆

Q **Why are Christmas trees like bad knitters?**

A **They both drop their needles**

☆✪☆✪☆✪☆✪☆

Q What happened when the snowgirl fell out with the snowboy?

A She gave him the cold shoulder

☆✪☆✪☆✪☆✪☆

Q **What's white, furry and smells minty?**

A **A polo bear!**

☆✪☆✪☆✪☆✪☆

Q What do snowmen wear on their heads?

A Ice caps

☆✪☆✪☆✪☆✪☆

Mad world

◉ What does a teddy bear put in his house?

🅐 Fur-niture

☆✪☆✪☆✪☆✪☆

◉ **Why are skunks always arguing?**

🅐 **Because they like to raise a stink!**

☆✪☆✪☆✪☆✪☆

◉ What was the first thing Queen Elizabeth did on ascending the throne?

🅐 Sit down!

☆✪☆✪☆✪☆✪☆

◉ **Why was there thunder and lightning in the laboratory?**

🅐 **The scientists were brainstorming!**

☆✪☆✪☆✪☆✪☆

◉ What did one wall say to the other?

🅐 I'll meet you at the corner

☆✪☆✪☆✪☆✪☆

◉ **Why did the boy tiptoe past the medicine cabinet?**

🅐 **He didn't want to wake the sleeping pills!**

☆✪☆✪☆✪☆✪☆

◉ How do angels greet each other?

🅰 They wave halo

☆✪☆✪☆✪☆✪☆

◉ **Why is perfume so obedient?**

🅰 **Because it's scent everywhere it goes**

☆✪☆✪☆✪☆✪☆

◉ What did the banana do when the monkey chased it?

🅰 The banana split

☆✪☆✪☆✪☆✪☆

◉ **Why does a hummingbird hum?**

🅰 **It doesn't know the words!**

◉ **What do you call a fish with no eyes?**

🅰 **A fsh**

☆✪☆✪☆✪☆✪☆

◉ What is black and white, black and white, black and white?

🅰 A zebra in a revolving door

Hilarious history

Q **Whose son was Edward, the Black Prince?**

A **Old King Coal**

☆✪☆✪☆✪☆✪☆

My teacher reminds me of history –

She's always repeating herself

☆✪☆✪☆✪☆✪☆

Q **What is a forum?**

A **Two-um plus two-um!**

☆✪☆✪☆✪☆✪☆

Q Why did Arthur have a round table?

A So no-one could corner him!

☆✪☆✪☆✪☆✪☆

Q **What was the greatest accomplishment of the ancient Romans?**

A **Speaking Latin!**

School daze

Teacher: Why do animals have fur coats?

Pupil: Because they would look silly in plastic macs, Sir!

☆✿☆✿☆✿☆✿☆

Teacher: Why are you picking your nose in class?

Pupil: My mother won't let me do it at home!

☆✿☆✿☆✿☆✿☆

"Here's my school report Dad."

"Well there's one thing in your favour, son. With grades like this you can't be cheating!"

Teacher: Charlie, please don't whistle while you're working.

Charlie: But I'm not working – just whistling!

☆✿☆✿☆✿☆✿☆

Teacher: Do you need a pocket calculator?

Pupil: No thanks. I know how many pockets I've got!

☆✿☆✿☆✿☆✿☆

Teacher: What happens to gold when it's exposed to the air?

Pupil: It gets stolen!

Going bananas

Q What happened when the chicken slept under the car?

A She woke up 'oily' next morning?

☆✪☆✪☆✪☆✪☆

Q **What's the best day of the week for sleeping?**

A **Snooze-day**

☆✪☆✪☆✪☆✪☆

Q **What gets bigger and bigger, the more you take away?**

A **A hole!**

☆✪☆✪☆✪☆✪☆

Q How do you make soup golden?

A Add 24 carrots?

☆✪☆✪☆✪☆✪☆

Q What toothpaste does Santa use?

A Crest'mas

☆✪☆✪☆✪☆✪☆

Q **Where does Tarzan buy his clothes?**

A **At a jungle sale!**

☆✪☆✪☆✪☆✪☆

◉ What do you get if you cross a giraffe and a rooster?

Ⓐ An animal who wakes up people who live on the top floor

☆✪☆✪☆✪☆✪☆

◉ **How do you know carrots are good for your eyes?**

Ⓐ **Because you never see rabbits wearing glasses!**

◉ **Why was Cinderella such a bad ice skater?**

Ⓐ **Because her coach was a pumpkin!**

☆✪☆✪☆✪☆✪☆

◉ What do you call two banana peels?

Ⓐ A pair of slippers

119

Good girls

Teacher: I'd like you to be very quiet today, class. I've got a dreadful headache.

Alice: Please, Miss! You should do what mum does when she has a headache.

Teacher: What's that?

Alice: She sends us out to play!

☆✪☆✪☆✪☆✪☆

◉ What did the zombie's friend say when he introduced him to his girlfriend?

🅰 Good grief! Where did you dig her up from?

☆✪☆✪☆✪☆✪☆

Lisa: Were any famous people born on your birthday?

Sarah: No, only little babies.

☆✪☆✪☆✪☆✪☆

Mary: Dad, that dentist wasn't painless like he advertised.

Father: Did he hurt you?

Mary: No, but he really screamed when I bit his finger!

Birthday bonanza

Natalie: I guess I didn't get my birthday wish.

Liz: How do you know?

Natalie: You're still here!

☆✪☆✪☆✪☆✪☆

⊙ What usually comes after the monster lights his birthday candles?

Ⓐ The fire brigade

☆✪☆✪☆✪☆✪☆

⊙ Where does a snowman put his birthday candles?

Ⓐ On his birthday flake!

⊙ Why did the boy feel warm on his birthday?

Ⓐ Because everyone was toasting him!

☆✪☆✪☆✪☆✪☆

Eric: I got a gold watch for my girlfriend.

Ernie: I wish I could get a swap like that!

☆✪☆✪☆✪☆✪☆

⊙ What party game do rabbits like to play?

Ⓐ Musical hares

Gag-tastic!

Q What season is it when you're on a trampoline?

A Spring time

☆✪☆✪☆✪☆✪☆

Q **What kind of music do mummies like?**

A **"Wrap" music**

☆✪☆✪☆✪☆✪☆

Q How do you repair a broken tomato?

A With tomato paste!

☆✪☆✪☆✪☆✪☆

Q **Why did the skeleton play the piano?**

A **Because he didn't have any organs!**

☆✪☆✪☆✪☆✪☆

Q What's full of holes but still holds water?

A A sponge

☆✪☆✪☆✪☆✪☆

Q **Why did the baby strawberry cry?**

A **His parents were in a jam!**

☆✪☆✪☆✪☆✪☆

A chicken goes into a library and says to the librarian, "Bawk!" in a high-pitched squawk. The librarian looks down, says "Oh, you want a book?" and gives the chicken a book. The chicken walks out with the book but is back in five minutes, drops the book in front of the librarian, and says, "Bawk, bawk." The librarian says, "Oh, you want two books?" and gives the chicken two books. The chicken walks out with the two books. Five minutes later, the chicken is back, drops the books, and says, "Bawk, bawk, bawk." The librarian says, "Oh, you want three books now?" and gives the chicken three books. The chicken walks out with the three books. This time the librarian follows the chicken to see where he is going. The chicken walks down to the pond below the library and drops the books, one at a time, in front of a big bullfrog. The frog looks at the books as they drop and says, in his deep bullfrog voice, "Red-it, red-it, red-it."

Q **What do you get if you cross a snake and a kangaroo?**

A **A skipping rope**

☆✪☆✪☆✪☆✪☆

Q What do you call a three-legged donkey?

A A wonkey!

Animal antics

Q What's grey and moves at a hundred miles an hour?

A A jet propelled elephant!

☆✪☆✪☆✪☆✪☆

Q What do you call a show full of lions?

A The mane event!

☆✪☆✪☆✪☆✪☆

Q What is a horse's favourite sport?

A Stable tennis!

Q What do you get if you cross a leopard with a watchdog?

A A terrified postman!

☆✪☆✪☆✪☆✪☆

Q How do hens dance?

A Chick-to-chick!

☆✪☆✪☆✪☆✪☆

"Who's been eating my porridge?"
squeaked Baby Bear.
"Who's been eating my porridge?"
cried Mother Bear.
"Burp!" said Father Bear.

☆✪☆✪☆✪☆✪☆

⊙ **What's red and dangerous?**

A **Strawberry and tarantula jelly!**

☆✪☆✪☆✪☆✪☆

⊙ What do you get from an Arctic cow?

A Ice cream!

☆✪☆✪☆✪☆✪☆

⊙ **What's big and grey and lives in a lake in Scotland?**

A **The Loch Ness Elephant!**

☆✪☆✪☆✪☆✪☆

⊙ How are tigers like sergeants in the army?

A They both wear stripes!

☆✪☆✪☆✪☆✪☆

Q Knock, knock!
Who's there?
Anita
Anita who?
turn over for answer!

Crazy as a coconut

Doctor, Doctor, I feel like a racehorse

Take one of these every four laps!

☆✪☆✪☆✪☆✪☆

◉ **What did one octopus say to the other octopus?**

🅐 **I want to hold your hand, hand, hand, hand, hand, hand, hand, hand**

☆✪☆✪☆✪☆✪☆

◉ **What do you call cheese that is not yours?**

🅐 **Nacho cheese**

☆✪☆✪☆✪☆✪☆

◉ What do you get if you cross a cat and a lemon?

🅐 A sour puss!

☆✪☆✪☆✪☆✪☆

◉ **What do you call someone who's afraid of Father Christmas?**

🅐 **Claus-trophobic!**

☆✪☆✪☆✪☆✪☆

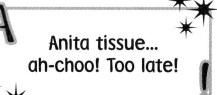

A Anita tissue...
ah-choo! Too late!

What do you call...

○ What do you call a man with a map on his head?

🅰 Miles

☆✪☆✪☆✪☆✪☆

○ What do you call a man with a paper bag on his head?

🅰 Russell

○ **What do you call a woman with a toilet on her head?**

🅰 **Lou**

☆✪☆✪☆✪☆✪☆

○ What do you call a woman with two toilets on her head?

🅰 Lulu

☆✪☆✪☆✪☆✪☆

○ **What do you call a man with a legal document on his head?**

🅰 **Will**

☆✪☆✪☆✪☆✪☆

Slapstick

Q How do trains hear?

A Through their engin-eers

☆✪☆✪☆✪☆✪☆

Q What do lawyers wear to court?

A Lawsuits!

☆✪☆✪☆✪☆✪☆

Q **Why did the scientist install a knocker on his door?**

A **He wanted to win the no-bell prize**

☆✪☆✪☆✪☆✪☆

Two fisherman are out sailing when suddenly a hand appears out of the water. "What's that?" asks the first fisherman, "It looks as if someone is drowning!" "No," explains the second fisherman, "it's just a little wave!"

☆✪☆✪☆✪☆✪☆

Q Why does a ballerina wear a tutu?

A Because a one-one's too small and a three-three's too big

☆✪☆✪☆✪☆✪☆

Q **What's an Eskimo's favourite song?**

A **Freeze a jolly good fellow!**

⊙ Where do snowmen put their web pages?

🅰 On the winter-net

☆✪☆✪☆✪☆✪☆

⊙ **Why was the belt sent to jail?**

🅰 **Because it held up a pair of trousers!**

☆✪☆✪☆✪☆✪☆

⊙ Who earns money by driving customers away?

🅰 A taxi-driver

☆✪☆✪☆✪☆✪☆

⊙ **Why did the idiot eat the candle?**

🅰 **He wanted a light snack!**

☆✪☆✪☆✪☆✪☆

⊙ What kind of bed does a mermaid sleep in?

🅰 A water bed!

Doctor, Doctor

Doctor, Doctor, I think I'm suffering from déjà vu!

Didn't I see you yesterday?

☆✪☆✪☆✪☆✪☆

Doctor, Doctor, I feel like a spoon!

Well sit still and don't stir

☆✪☆✪☆✪☆✪☆

Doctor, Doctor, I keep thinking I'm a woodworm

How boring for you!

☆✪☆✪☆✪☆✪☆

Doctor, Doctor, I'm on a diet and it's making me irritable. Yesterday I bit someone's ear off

Oh dear, that's a lot of calories!

☆✪☆✪☆✪☆✪☆

Doctor, Doctor, I think I need glasses

You certainly do Sir, this is a fish and chip shop!

Animal antics

- **Q** What did the lion tell his cubs when he taught them to hunt?

- **A** Don't cross the road 'til you see the zebra crossing

☆✪☆✪☆✪☆✪☆

- **Q** **What's the difference between a cat and a flea?**

- **A** **A cat can have fleas but a flea can't have cats!**

☆✪☆✪☆✪☆✪☆

- **Q** What do you get if you cross a parrot and a centipede?

- **A** A walkie talkie

☆✪☆✪☆✪☆✪☆

- **Q** **What happened when the chef found a daddy-long-legs in his salad?**

- **A** **It became a daddy-short-legs!**

☆✪☆✪☆✪☆✪☆

- **Q** Why did the spider buy a car?

- **A** So he could take it for a spin!

☆✪☆✪☆✪☆✪☆

- **Q** **How do you keep flies out of the kitchen?**

- **A** **Put a pile of manure in the living room!**

Bonkers!

Joe: What did you get for Christmas?

Ian: A mouthorgan, it's the best present I've ever had!

Joe: Why's that?

Ian: My mum gives me extra pocket money every week not to play it.

☆✪☆✪☆✪☆✪☆

◉ What steps would you take if a madman came running towards you?

🅰 Great big ones!

☆✪☆✪☆✪☆✪☆

◉ Did you hear about the stupid Kamikaze pilot?

🅰 He flew 57 missions

☆✪☆✪☆✪☆✪☆

◉ How did Noah see the animals on the Ark at night?

🅰 By flood lighting

☆✪☆✪☆✪☆✪☆

Nick: How old is your granddad?

Andy: I don't know but we've had him for ages.

☆✪☆✪☆✪☆✪☆

Michael: I was in a play called "Breakfast in Bed" last year.

Mandy: Did you have a big role?

Michael: No, just toast and marmalade.

☆✪☆✪☆✪☆✪☆

Q What washes up on very small beaches?

A Microwaves

Q What do you call a foreign body in a chip pan?

A An Unidentified Frying Object

☆✪☆✪☆✪☆✪☆

Q What do you get if you cross a Scottish legend and a bad egg?

A The Loch Ness Pongster

Going bananas

Q What do you call a cow eating grass?

A A lawn moo-er

☆✪☆✪☆✪☆✪☆

Doctor, Doctor, I can't get to sleep

Sit on the edge of the bed and you'll soon drop off

☆✪☆✪☆✪☆✪☆

Q Why did the baby cookie cry?

A Because its mother was a wafer so long

☆✪☆✪☆✪☆✪☆

Q What's white, fluffy and beats its chest?

A A meringue-utan

☆✪☆✪☆✪☆✪☆

Q What did the whirlwind say to the car?

A Do you want to go for a spin?

☆✪☆✪☆✪☆✪☆

Q Why did the farmer name his pig Ink?

A Because it kept running out of the pen!

☆✪☆✪☆✪☆✪☆

Mel: I've been e-mailing William Shakespeare.

Jason: Shakespeare's dead, silly.

Mel: No wonder he hasn't replied!

☆✪☆✪☆✪☆✪☆

⊙ **What's the best way to speak to a monster?**

🅰 **From a long distance**

☆✪☆✪☆✪☆✪☆

⊙ How do you stop a skunk from smelling?

🅰 Put a peg on its nose!

☆✪☆✪☆✪☆✪☆

⊙ **What did the bug say when it hit the windscreen?**

🅰 **I don't have the guts to do that again!**

☆✪☆✪☆✪☆✪☆

⊙ What's green, has six legs, and hurts when it falls out of a tree on you?

🅰 A snooker table

Ghoulishly funny

Q **Why did the ghost go to the doctor?**

A **To get a boo-ster shot**

☆✪☆✪☆✪☆✪☆

Q What does a polite monster say when he sees you for the first time?

A Pleased to eat you!

☆✪☆✪☆✪☆✪☆

Q **Did you hear about the mad vampire?**

A **He went a little batty**

☆✪☆✪☆✪☆✪☆

"Try to be nice to mother when she visits this weekend dear," Mrs Monster said to Mr Monster. "Fall down when she hits you!"

☆✪☆✪☆✪☆✪☆

Q **What's big, heavy, furry, dangerous and has 16 wheels?**

A **A monster on roller-skates**

Mad world

Q **How can you make seven an even number?**

A **Remove the "S"**

☆✪☆✪☆✪☆✪☆

Q What do you call someone that keeps talking when no one is listening?

A A teacher!

☆✪☆✪☆✪☆✪☆

Q **Why did the dolphin cross the beach?**

A **To get to the other tide**

☆✪☆✪☆✪☆✪☆

Q What kind of cake do you get for school dinners?

A A stomach-cake!

☆✪☆✪☆✪☆✪☆

Q **Why was Santa's little helper depressed?**

A **Because he had low elf esteem**

☆✪☆✪☆✪☆✪☆

Q Why did the idiot put a clock under his desk?

A Because he wanted to work over-time!

Hilarious history

Q Where did the Romans land when they first arrived in Britain?

A On their feet!

☆✪☆✪☆✪☆✪☆

Mother: Why are you doing so badly in history?

Son: The teacher keeps asking about things that happened before I was born!

☆✪☆✪☆✪☆✪☆

Q Where was the Magna Carta signed?

A At the bottom!

☆✪☆✪☆✪☆✪☆

Q Why were the dark ages called the dark ages?

A Because there were so many knights!

☆✪☆✪☆✪☆✪☆

Q If Atlas supported the world on his shoulders, then who supported Atlas?

A His wife!

☆✪☆✪☆✪☆✪☆

Lady: We had wild boar for dinner last night.

Knight: Wild?

Lady: Well, he wasn't happy about it!

Teacher: Who can tell me where Hadrian's Wall is?

Pupil: Around Hadrian's garden, Miss!

☆✪☆✪☆✪☆✪☆

☉ Who succeeded the first President of the USA?

Ⓐ The second one!

☆✪☆✪☆✪☆✪☆

1st Roman Soldier: What's the time?

2nd Roman Soldier: XX past VII!

☆✪☆✪☆✪☆✪☆

☉ What was Camelot famous for?

Ⓐ It's knight life!

☉ What did Noah do while spending time on the Ark?

Ⓐ Fished, but he didn't catch much. He only had two worms!

☆✪☆✪☆✪☆✪☆

☉ Why did the knight run around asking for a tin opener?

Ⓐ He had a bee in his suit of armour!

Gag-tastic!

⊙ What did the decorator say to the wall?

🅰 One more crack like that and I'll plaster you!

☆✪☆✪☆✪☆✪☆

⊙ **What is an astronaut's favourite part of a computer?**

🅰 **The space bar!**

☆✪☆✪☆✪☆✪☆

⊙ Did you hear about the two men that walked into a bar?

🅰 It was careless really, the second man should have seen it

☆✪☆✪☆✪☆✪☆

⊙ **How does the sea say hello to the beach?**

🅰 **It waves**

☆✪☆✪☆✪☆✪☆

Mrs Smith and her small daughter Carol were outside the church watching all the comings and goings of a wedding. After all the excitement was over Carol said to her mother, "Why did the bride change her mind, Mummy?"
"What do you mean, change her mind?" asked Mrs Smith.
"Well," said Carol, "she went into the church with one man and came out with another!"

☆✪☆✪☆✪☆✪☆

◉ What flower grows between your nose and your chin?

🅐 Tulips

☆✪☆✪☆✪☆✪☆

◉ Why did the chicken cross the playground?

🅐 To get to the other slide

◉ What do you take off last before getting into bed?

🅐 Your feet off the floor

☆✪☆✪☆✪☆✪☆

Doctor, Doctor, I think I'm a bridge

What's come over you?

Four cars, two lorrys and a bike!

Animal antics

Q Why do you never see zebras at Kings Cross?

A Because it's a 'mane-lion' station!

☆✪☆✪☆✪☆✪☆

Q **What's the difference between an elephant and a bad pupil?**

A **One rarely bites and the other barely writes!**

☆✪☆✪☆✪☆✪☆

Q Why shouldn't you play poker in the jungle?

A There are too many cheetahs!

☆✪☆✪☆✪☆✪☆

Q **What are spiders' webs good for?**

A **Spiders of course!**

☆✪☆✪☆✪☆✪☆

Q Why was the farmer hopping mad?

A Because someone trod on his corn!

☆✪☆✪☆✪☆✪☆

Q **What's grey with red spots?**

A **An elephant with measles**

☆✪☆✪☆✪☆✪☆

⊙ Why don't centipedes play football?

🅰 Because by the time they've got their boots on it's time to go home!

☆✪☆✪☆✪☆✪☆

⊙ **Why were the flies playing football in a saucer?**

🅰 **They where playing for the cup!**

☆✪☆✪☆✪☆✪☆

⊙ What do you call the story of The Three Little Pigs?

🅰 A pigtail!

☆✪☆✪☆✪☆✪☆

⊙ **Why did the rooster cross the road?**

🅰 **To cockadoodle-dooo something**

☆✪☆✪☆✪☆✪☆

⊙ What's grey, has four legs and jumps up and down?

🅰 An elephant on a trampoline!

Doctor, Doctor

Doctor, Doctor, I've got wind! Can you give me something?

Yes – here's a kite!

☆✪☆✪☆✪☆✪☆

Doctor, Doctor, you've taken out my tonsils, my gall bladder, my varicose veins and my appendix, but I still don't feel well!

That's quite enough out of you!

☆✪☆✪☆✪☆✪☆

Doctor, Doctor, I keep seeing double

Please sit on the couch

Which one!

Doctor, Doctor, everyone thinks I'm a liar

Well I can't believe that!

☆✪☆✪☆✪☆✪☆

Doctor, Doctor, my baby is the image of me

Never mind just so long as he's healthy!

Slapstick

Q **Why are pianos so hard to open?**

A **The keys are inside**

☆✪☆✪☆✪☆✪☆

Q Why did Jimmy throw the clock out of the window?

A Because he wanted to see time fly!

☆✪☆✪☆✪☆✪☆

Q Why is an empty purse always the same?

A Because there's never any change in it

☆✪☆✪☆✪☆✪☆

Q **What happens to a hamburger that misses a lot of school?**

A **He has a lot of ketchup time!**

☆✪☆✪☆✪☆✪☆

Q What's worse than raining cats and dogs?

A Hailing taxis

Q **Knock, knock!**
Who's there?
Justin
Justin who?
turn over for answer!

Crazy as a coconut

A little boy came running into the kitchen. "Dad, dad," he said, "there's a monster at the door with a really ugly face."
"Tell him you've already got one," said his father!

☆✪☆✪☆✪☆✪☆

◉ What nails do carpenters hate hitting?

🅐 Fingernails

☆✪☆✪☆✪☆✪☆

A
Just-in time
for dinner!

◉ Did you hear the joke about the roof?

🅐 Never mind, it'll only go over your head!

☆✪☆✪☆✪☆✪☆

◉ Why did the turtle cross the road?

🅐 To get to the Shell station!

☆✪☆✪☆✪☆✪☆

◉ What's the difference between a jeweller and a prison guard?

🅐 One sells watches and the other watches cells

☆✪☆✪☆✪☆✪☆

⊙ What starts with a P, ends with an E and has a million letters in it?

🅰 Post Office!

☆✪☆✪☆✪☆✪☆

⊙ **What does a bee use to brush its hair?**

🅰 **A honeycomb!**

☆✪☆✪☆✪☆✪☆

"It's a pity you've gone on hunger strike," said the convict's girlfriend on visiting day

"Why's that?"

"I've put a file in your cake!"

☆✪☆✪☆✪☆✪☆

⊙ **What do computers eat when they get hungry?**

🅰 **Chips!**

☆✪☆✪☆✪☆✪☆

⊙ What do you call a blind dinosaur?

🅰 I-don't-think-he-saurus

Fit for fun

Q What is black and white and black and white and black and white?

A A Newcastle fan rolling down a hill!

☆✪☆✪☆✪☆✪☆

Q Why was the struggling manager seen shaking his cat?

A To see if there was any more money in the kitty!

☆✪☆✪☆✪☆✪☆

Q What part of a sports stadium is never the same?

A The changing rooms!

☆✪☆✪☆✪☆✪☆

Q Which football team loves ice-cream?

A Aston Vanilla!

☆✪☆✪☆✪☆✪☆

Referee: I'm sending you off!

Player: What for?

Referee: The rest of the match.

☆✪☆✪☆✪☆✪☆

Q Which insect is terrible in goal?

A The fumble bee!

☆✪☆✪☆✪☆✪☆

Q Which player helps to keep up the fuel supply?

A Paul gas-coin!

☆✪☆✪☆✪☆✪☆

Q Did you hear about the team who ate too much pudding?

A They got jelly-gated!

☆✪☆✪☆✪☆✪☆

Q What is a goalie's favourite snack?

A Beans on post!

☆✪☆✪☆✪☆✪☆

Q What tea do footballers drink?

A Penal-tea!

Q Why do birds sell so quickly when they come up on the transfer market?

A They tend to go cheep!

☆✪☆✪☆✪☆✪☆

Q How do chickens encourage their teams?

A They egg them on!

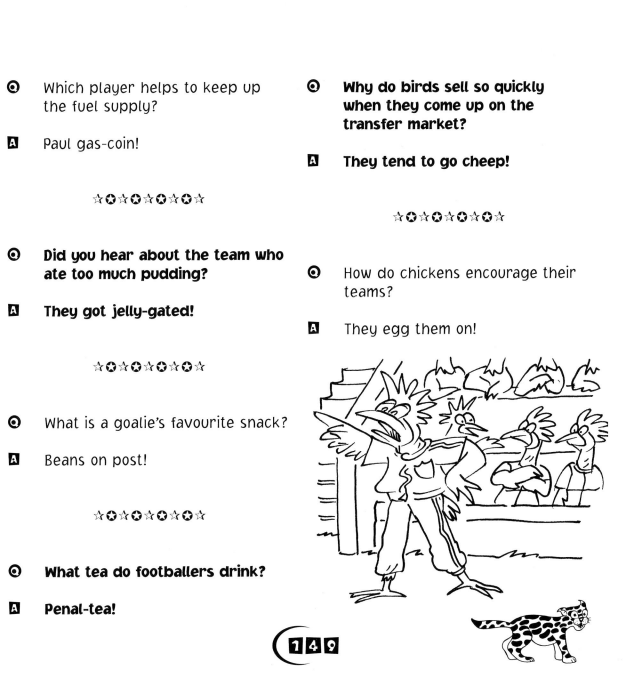

Out of this world!

Q **Why did Captain Kirk go into the ladies toilet?**

A **To boldly go where no man has gone before**

☆✪☆✪☆✪☆✪☆

Q What kind of tics do you find on the Moon?

A Luna-tics!

☆✪☆✪☆✪☆✪☆

Q **What did the metric alien say?**

A **"Take me to your litre!"**

☆✪☆✪☆✪☆✪☆

Q What do you call a space magician?

A A flying sorcerer

☆✪☆✪☆✪☆✪☆

Q **What did the alien say to the petrol pump?**

A **"Don't you know it's rude to stick your finger in your ear when I'm talking to you!"**

Terrible teachers

Teacher: What is the plural of mouse?

Pupil: Mice.

Teacher: Good, now what's the plural of baby?

Pupil: Twins!

☆✪☆✪☆✪☆✪☆

Teacher: What family does the octopus belong to?

Pupil: Nobody I know!

☆✪☆✪☆✪☆✪☆

⊙ **Why did the teacher become an electrician?**

🅐 **For a bit of light relief**

Teacher: This is the fifth time I've had to tell you off this week, what have you got to say about that?

Pupil: Thank heavens it's Friday!

☆✪☆✪☆✪☆✪☆

Teacher: If you add 47,693 to 58,679, divide the answer by 7 and times by 3, what do you get?

Pupil: The wrong answer!

☆✪☆✪☆✪☆✪☆

Teacher: I want you to tell me the longest sentence you can think of.

Pupil: Life imprisonment.

151

Going bananas

⊙ **Why did the elephant stand on the marshmallow?**

🄰 **So he wouldn't fall into the hot chocolate**

☆✪☆✪☆✪☆✪☆

⊙ What did one volcano say to the other volcano?

🄰 "I lava you."

☆✪☆✪☆✪☆✪☆

⊙ **Why do some fish live at the bottom of the ocean?**

🄰 **Because they dropped out of school!**

☆✪☆✪☆✪☆✪☆

⊙ Did you hear the joke about the pack of cards?

🄰 It's no big deal

☆✪☆✪☆✪☆✪☆

⊙ **What is a lion's favourite food?**

🄰 **Baked beings**

☆✪☆✪☆✪☆✪☆

⊙ Why do hens never get rich?

🄰 Because they work for chicken feed

☆✪☆✪☆✪☆✪☆

Slapstick

Q   Why did the monster dye his hair yellow?

A   He wanted to see if blondes have more fun

☆✪☆✪☆✪☆✪☆

Teacher: Charlie, I'm glad to see your handwriting has improved.

Charlie: Thank you Sir.

Charlie: Unfortunately, now I can see how bad your spelling is!

☆✪☆✪☆✪☆✪☆

Q   What did the light say when it was turned off?

A   I'm delighted

Q   How does a lion greet the other animals?

A   "Pleased to eat you!"

☆✪☆✪☆✪☆✪☆

Peter: This morning my dad gave me soap flakes instead of corn flakes for breakfast.

Mickey: I bet you were mad.

Peter: Mad? I was foaming at the mouth!

⊙ **What happened when the wheel was invented?**

🄰 **It caused a revolution**

☆✪☆✪☆✪☆✪☆

⊙ What happened to the man who tried to cross a lion with a goat?

🄰 He had to get a new goat!

☆✪☆✪☆✪☆✪☆

Teacher: What came after the Stone Age and the Bronze Age?

Pupil: The saus-age?

☆✪☆✪☆✪☆✪☆

⊙ What do you give an elephant with big feet?

🄰 Plenty of room

☆✪☆✪☆✪☆✪☆

⊙ **Why didn't the clock work?**

🄰 **Because it needed a hand**

☆✪☆✪☆✪☆✪☆

⊙ Who invented fractions?

🄰 Henry the $\frac{1}{8}$th!

☆✪☆✪☆✪☆✪☆

⊙ **How long does it take for a candle to burn down?**

🄰 **About a wick!**

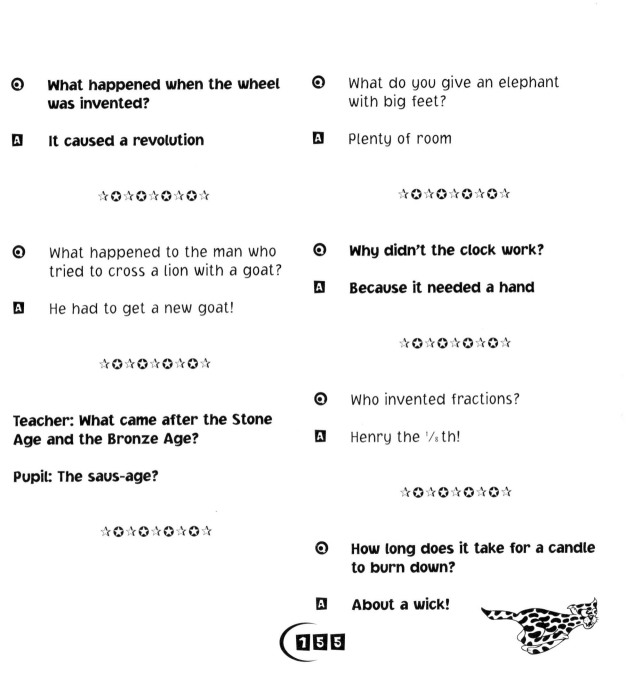

School daze

Teacher: I thought I told you to stand at the end of the line?

Pupil: I tried, but there was someone already there.

☆✪☆✪☆✪☆✪☆

Teacher: If there are twelve flies on a desk and I hit one with a ruler, how many are left?

Pupil: Just the squashed one!

☆✪☆✪☆✪☆✪☆

Teacher: What a sad face, what would you say if I came to school with a face like that?

Pupil: I'd be too polite to mention it!

◉ What's the difference between a railway guard and a teacher?

🅰 One minds the train and the other trains the mind!

☆✪☆✪☆✪☆✪☆

Teacher: Can you tell me something important that didn't exist 100 years ago?

Pupil: Me!

☆✪☆✪☆✪☆✪☆

Teacher: Does anyone know which month has 28 days?

Pupil: All of them.

☆✪☆✪☆✪☆✪☆

Animal antics

◉ **What's grey and goes round and round?**

🅐 **An elephant in a washing machine!**

☆✪☆✪☆✪☆✪☆

◉ Why do birds fly south in winter?

🅐 Because it's too far to walk!

◉ Why does a stork stand on one leg?

🅐 Because it would fall over if it lifted the other one!

☆✪☆✪☆✪☆✪☆

◉ **What do tigers wear in bed?**

🅐 **Stripy pyjamas!**

Gag-tastic!

- ⊙ **What goes up when the rain comes down?**

- 🅰 **An umbrella**

☆✪☆✪☆✪☆✪☆

- ⊙ What do you do with a blue whale?

- 🅰 Try to cheer him up!

☆✪☆✪☆✪☆✪☆

"Mum, teacher was asking me today if I have any brothers or sisters."

"That's nice of her to take an interest. What did she say when you told her you were an only child?"

She just said, "Thank goodness!"

- ⊙ Where was King Solomon's temple?

- 🅰 On his forehead

☆✪☆✪☆✪☆✪☆

Joe: My dog plays chess.

Gerard: Wow! He must be clever!

Joe: Not really, he hasn't beaten me once!

Techno ticklers

◉ Why was the computer so thin?

🅰 Because it hadn't had many bytes!

☆✪☆✪☆✪☆✪☆

PE Teacher: Why did you kick that ball at the computer?

Pupil: You told me to put it in the Net!

☆✪☆✪☆✪☆✪☆

Tom: I've been on my computer all night.

Charlie: Wouldn't you be more comfortable on a bed like everyone else?

☆✪☆✪☆✪☆✪☆

◉ **Why didn't the boy mouse get on with the girl mouse?**

🅰 **They just didn't click**

☆✪☆✪☆✪☆✪☆

◉ When do spooks get a chance to use the computer?

🅰 Whenever the ghost is clear

☆✪☆✪☆✪☆✪☆

Pupil: I've been sitting at this computer for ages and I haven't seen a single website.

Teacher: That's because you're supposed to sit facing the screen!

Hilarious history

Q **Why did Eve want to move to New York?**

A **She fell for the Big Apple!**

☆✪☆✪☆✪☆✪☆

Q Who invented King Arthur's round table?

A Sir Cumference!

☆✪☆✪☆✪☆✪☆

Q **Why did Henry VIII have so many wives?**

A **He liked to chop and change!**

☆✪☆✪☆✪☆✪☆

Q How did Christopher Columbus's men sleep on their ships?

A With their eyes shut!

☆✪☆✪☆✪☆✪☆

Q **Where did knights learn to kill dragons?**

A **At knight school!**

Ghoulishly funny

Q Why are there fences around cemeteries?

A Because people are dying to get in

☆✪☆✪☆✪☆✪☆

Q **Who won the Monster Beauty Contest?**

A **No one!**

☆✪☆✪☆✪☆✪☆

Did you know that Dracula wants to become a comedian?

He's looking for a crypt writer

☆✪☆✪☆✪☆✪☆

Q **Why was the big, hairy, two-headed monster top of the class at school?**

A **Because two heads are better than one**

☆✪☆✪☆✪☆✪☆

Q What type of coffee do vampires prefer?

A De-coffinated!

☆✪☆✪☆✪☆✪☆

Q **Who did Frankenstein take on a date?**

A **His ghoul friend**

Bonkers!

Alice: Did you hear about the scientist who invented a gas that could burn through anything?

Clare: No, what happened?

Alice: Now he's trying to invent something to hold it in!

☆✪☆✪☆✪☆✪☆

⊙ What cheese is made backwards?

🅰 Edam

☆✪☆✪☆✪☆✪☆

⊙ **What do cannibals eat for breakfast?**

🅰 **Buttered host**

Dad: It's time for your violin lesson.

Son: Oh, fiddle!

☆✪☆✪☆✪☆✪☆

Charlie: What did Daddy say when he fell in the dung heap?

Tom: Shall I leave out the swear words?

Charlie: Yes.

Tom: He didn't say anything!

Christmas goodies

Q What do you get if you cross an apple and a Christmas tree?

A A pineapple!

☆✪☆✪☆✪☆✪☆

Q **Why did the reindeer wear black boots?**

A **Because his brown ones were all muddy!**

☆✪☆✪☆✪☆✪☆

Q What do reindeer have that no other animals do?

A Baby reindeer!

☆✪☆✪☆✪☆✪☆

Q **What stays hot even at the North Pole?**

A **Mustard!**

☆✪☆✪☆✪☆✪☆

Q What did the big candle say to the little candle?

A I'm going out tonight

☆✪☆✪☆✪☆✪☆

Q **What's the difference between a biscuit and a reindeer?**

A **You can't dunk a reindeer in your tea!**

Mad world

⊙ What question can't be answered with a yes?

🅐 Are you asleep?

☆✪☆✪☆✪☆✪☆

⊙ **Why did Robin Hood rob the rich?**

🅐 **Because the poor didn't have anything worth stealing!**

☆✪☆✪☆✪☆✪☆

⊙ What do you give a train driver for Christmas?

🅐 Platform shoes!

☆✪☆✪☆✪☆✪☆

Teacher: Why have you got cotton wool in your ears?

Pupil: Well you said things go in one ear and out the other so I'm trying to keep them all in!

☆✪☆✪☆✪☆✪☆

⊙ Why was the lion-tamer fined?

🅐 He parked on a yellow lion!

☆✪☆✪☆✪☆✪☆

⊙ **What has a bottom at the top?**

🅐 **Your legs**

☆✪☆✪☆✪☆✪☆

Q Why did the picture go to jail?

A It was framed!

☆✪☆✪☆✪☆✪☆

Q Which dinosaur has four legs and flies?

A A dead one!

Q What's big and grey and wears a mask?

A The ele-phantom of the opera!

☆✪☆✪☆✪☆✪☆

Monster: When I grow up I want to be a bus driver.

Witch: Well, I won't stand in your way.

Ghoulishly funny

⊙ **Why did the mummy call the doctor?**

🅰 **Because of the coffin**

☆✪☆✪☆✪☆✪☆

⊙ What do you give a monster with big feet?

🅰 Big flippers

☆✪☆✪☆✪☆✪☆

⊙ **What did the monster do to stop his son biting his nails?**

🅰 **He cut all his fingers off!**

☆✪☆✪☆✪☆✪☆

⊙ Why are vampire families so close?

🅰 Because blood is thicker than water

☆✪☆✪☆✪☆✪☆

⊙ **How do you stop a monster digging up your garden?**

🅰 **Take his spade away**

Crazy as a coconut

Why did the traffic light turn red?

You would too if you had to change in the middle of the street!

☆✪☆✪☆✪☆✪☆

Have you heard the joke about the butter?

I better not tell you, you'll only spread it

☆✪☆✪☆✪☆✪☆

Knock, knock!
Who's there?
Cows
Cows who?
turn over for answer!

What does a dentist call his x-rays?

Tooth-pics

☆✪☆✪☆✪☆✪☆

Where do cows go on holiday?

Moo York

☆✪☆✪☆✪☆✪☆

Why was the elephant late for the plane?

He forgot his trunk

☆✪☆✪☆✪☆✪☆

Techno ticklers

◉ What sits in the middle of the World Wide Web?

A A very, very big spider!

☆✪☆✪☆✪☆✪☆

◉ Why do church bells never send e-mails?

A They'd rather give each other a ring

☆✪☆✪☆✪☆✪☆

Pupil: In other schools, pupils get a choice of computers to use.

Teacher: You get a choice here, too. Use the one we've got or don't use any at all.

☆✪☆✪☆✪☆✪☆

◉ Why don't you stamp e-mails?

A Because your foot would go through the screen!

☆✪☆✪☆✪☆✪☆

◉ Why did the mummy stop using the Internet?

A He was getting too wrapped up in it

No they don't, they moo!

Doctor, Doctor

Doctor, Doctor, my son has swallowed a roll of film!

Hmmm. Let's hope nothing develops

☆✪☆✪☆✪☆✪☆

Doctor, Doctor, You've got to help me – my hands won't stop shaking

Do you drink a lot?

Not really - I spill most of it!

Doctor, Doctor, how can I cure my sleep walking?

Sprinkle drawing pins on your bedroom floor!

☆✪☆✪☆✪☆✪☆

Doctor, Doctor, I dream there are monsters under my bed, what can I do?

Saw the legs off of your bed!

☆✪☆✪☆✪☆✪☆

Doctor, Doctor, will this ointment clear up my spots?

I never make rash promises!

Slapstick

Q How do you tell the difference between an elephant and a mouse?

A Try picking them up!

☆✪☆✪☆✪☆✪☆

Q **What starts with T, ends with T and is full of T?**

A **A teapot**

☆✪☆✪☆✪☆✪☆

Doctor, Doctor, people keep throwing garbage at me

Don't talk rubbish!

☆✪☆✪☆✪☆✪☆

Q **What gets wetter when it dries?**

A **A towel**

☆✪☆✪☆✪☆✪☆

Customer: I think I've got a bug in my computer.

Repairman: Does your computer make a humming noise?

Customer: Yes.

Repairman: Then it must be a humbug!

☆✪☆✪☆✪☆✪☆

Q **What was King Arthur's favourite game?**

A **Knights and crosses**

- Q Why did the bully kick the class computer?

- A The teacher told him to boot up the system

☆✪☆✪☆✪☆✪☆

A man rushed in to see the doctor and shouted, "Doctor! I think I'm shrinking!" The doctor said, "Now, settle down. You'll just have to be a little patient."

☆✪☆✪☆✪☆✪☆

- Q **What kind of boat pulls Dracula when he water skis?**

- A **A blood vessel**

- Q Why wouldn't they let the butterfly into the dance?

- A Because it was a moth ball

Animal antics

How do you milk a mouse?

You can't, the bucket won't fit underneath!

☆✪☆✪☆✪☆✪☆

What's grey and highly dangerous?

An elephant with a machine gun!

☆✪☆✪☆✪☆✪☆

How do you stop a rooster waking you up on Sunday?

Eat him on Saturday!

☆✪☆✪☆✪☆✪☆

What do you get if you cross a cow and a tadpole?

A bullfrog!

☆✪☆✪☆✪☆✪☆

How many skunks does it take to make a big stink?

A phew!

Fit for fun

⊙ When fish play football, who's the captain?

🅰 The team's kipper!

☆✪☆✪☆✪☆✪☆

⊙ **What is a bank manager's favourite type of football?**

🅰 **Fiver-side!**

☆✪☆✪☆✪☆✪☆

⊙ Why don't grasshoppers go to many rugby games?

🅰 They prefer cricket matches!

☆✪☆✪☆✪☆✪☆

⊙ **Where do football directors go when they are fed up?**

🅰 **The bored room!**

☆✪☆✪☆✪☆✪☆

⊙ What's the chilliest ground in the Premiership?

🅰 Cold Trafford!

☆✪☆✪☆✪☆✪☆

⊙ **Which football team do most cowboys support**

🅰 **Spurs**

☆✪☆✪☆✪☆✪☆

School daze

Teacher: Make up a sentence using the word lettuce, Mary.

Mary: Lettuce out of school early!

☆✪☆✪☆✪☆✪☆

Teacher: Daniel, can you tell me who broke the sound barrier?

Daniel: It wasn't me, honest!

☆✪☆✪☆✪☆✪☆

Father: I can't believe you've got four Ds and a C on your report.

Son: Maybe I concentrated too much on the one subject!

☆✪☆✪☆✪☆✪☆

Pupil: The music teacher didn't like what I was making today.

Dad: Why, what were you making?

Pupil: A racket!

☆✪☆✪☆✪☆✪☆

◉ Why did the maths teacher take a ruler to bed with him?

🅰 He wanted to see how long he would sleep

☆✪☆✪☆✪☆✪☆

Teacher: Ellen, I hope I didn't see you copying from Lucy's work?

Ellen: I hope you didn't too!

Teacher: Give me a sentence with the words defence, defeat and detail in it.

Pupil: When a horse jumps over defence, defeat go before detail!

☆✪☆✪☆✪☆✪☆

Teacher: Why are you the only child in class today?

Pupil: Because I was the only one who didn't have school dinners yesterday!

☆✪☆✪☆✪☆✪☆

Teacher: The word politics – can you give me an example of how to use it?

Pupil: My parrot swallowed a watch and now Polly ticks!

☆✪☆✪☆✪☆✪☆

Teacher: Why are you reading the last page of your history book first?

Pupil: I want to see how it ends!

☆✪☆✪☆✪☆✪☆

Teacher: What are you doing, crawling into school ten minutes late?

Pupil: Well you told me never to walk into school ten minutes late!

Doctor, Doctor

Doctor, Doctor, I've got foul breath and smelly feet

Sounds like you've got Foot and Mouth disease!

☆✪☆✪☆✪☆✪☆

Doctor, Doctor, When I press with my finger here... it hurts, and here... it hurts, and here... and here... What do you think is wrong with me?

You have a broken finger!

☆✪☆✪☆✪☆✪☆

Doctor, Doctor, I'm boiling up!

Just simmer down!

☆✪☆✪☆✪☆✪☆

Doctor, Doctor, I'm becoming invisible

Yes, I can see you're not all there!

☆✪☆✪☆✪☆✪☆

Doctor: You seem to be in excellent health. Your pulse is as regular as clockwork!

Patient: That's because you've got your hand on my watch!

Going bananas

⊙ **What do you call a very popular perfume?**

🅰 **A best-smeller**

☆✪☆✪☆✪☆✪☆

⊙ How does a leopard change its spots?

🅰 When it gets tired of one spot it just moves to another!

☆✪☆✪☆✪☆✪☆

⊙ **What do you call a pig with three eyes?**

🅰 **A piiig**

☆✪☆✪☆✪☆✪☆

⊙ What's invisible and smells like carrots?

🅰 Bunny farts!

☆✪☆✪☆✪☆✪☆

⊙ **What's green and loud?**

🅰 **A froghorn**

☆✪☆✪☆✪☆✪☆

⊙ What disappears when you stand up?

🅰 Your lap

☆✪☆✪☆✪☆✪☆

Birthday bonanza!

Anita: This birthday cake certainly is crunchy.

Cindy: Maybe you should spit out the plate!

☆✪☆✪☆✪☆✪☆

◉ Where do you find a birthday present for a cat?

🅰 In a cat-alogue!

☆✪☆✪☆✪☆✪☆

For his birthday the monster asked for a heavy sweater. So his friends gave him a sumo wrestler!

☆✪☆✪☆✪☆✪☆

◉ When is a birthday cake like a golf ball?

🅰 When it's been sliced

☆✪☆✪☆✪☆✪☆

◉ Why couldn't prehistoric man send birthday cards?

🅰 The stamps kept falling off the rocks!

Cathy: Is your dad getting older and wiser?

Alison: No, he's getting older and wider!

☆✪☆✪☆✪☆✪☆

What do cats like eating on their birthday?

A **Jelly and mice-cream!**

☆✪☆✪☆✪☆✪☆

Karl: I got my wife a VCP for her birthday.

John: Don't you mean a VCR?

Karl: No, a VCP ... Very Cheap Present!

☆✪☆✪☆✪☆✪☆

What's the difference between a stupid monster and a birthday candle?

A **The candle is a thousand times brighter!**

☆✪☆✪☆✪☆✪☆

Michelle: Did you go shopping for my birthday present?

Sally: Yeah, and I found the perfect thing.

Michelle: What thing is that?

Sally: Nothing!

☆✪☆✪☆✪☆✪☆

What's an elf's favourite cake?

A **Shortcake!**

Fit for fun

⊙ **What did the footballer say when he burped during a game?**

🅰 **Sorry, it was a freak hic!**

☆✪☆✪☆✪☆✪☆

⊙ Where do old bowling balls end up?

🅰 In the gutter!

☆✪☆✪☆✪☆✪☆

⊙ **Why are artists no good at football?**

🅰 **They keep drawing!**

☆✪☆✪☆✪☆✪☆

⊙ What do a footballer and a magician have in common?

🅰 Both love hat-tricks!

☆✪☆✪☆✪☆✪☆

⊙ **Why did the chicken get sent off?**

🅰 **For persistent fowl play!**

Crazy as a coconut

Q Why did the man with one hand cross the road?

A To get to the second-hand shop

☆✪☆✪☆✪☆✪☆

Q Why is tennis such a loud game?

A Because each player raises a racquet

☆✪☆✪☆✪☆✪☆

Q Why did the boy eat his homework?

A Because his teacher said it was a piece of cake!

☆✪☆✪☆✪☆✪☆

The lifeguard at the public swimming pool approaches little Tommy. "You're not allowed to pee in the pool," said the life guard. "I'm going to report you." "But everyone pees in the pool," said Tommy.
"Not from the diving board!"

☆✪☆✪☆✪☆✪☆

Q How can you get a set of teeth put in for free?

A Hit a lion!

☆✪☆✪☆✪☆✪☆

Q What did the ground say to the earthquake?

A You crack me up!

Bonkers!

Q Which cake wanted to rule the world?

A Atilla the Bun

☆✪☆✪☆✪☆✪☆

Smith: I hate to tell you this, but your wife just fell down the wishing well.

Jones: I can't believe it worked!

☆✪☆✪☆✪☆✪☆

Q What happens when plumbers die?

A They go down the drain

☆✪☆✪☆✪☆✪☆

Mum: Eat up your spinach, it'll put colour in your cheeks.

Son: But, I don't want green cheeks!

☆✪☆✪☆✪☆✪☆

Sarah: Why do you keep doing the backstroke?

Belinda: I've just had lunch and don't want to swim on a full stomach!

☆✪☆✪☆✪☆✪☆

Matt: What do you mean by telling everyone that I'm an idiot?

Paul: I'm sorry, I didn't know it was supposed to be a secret!

☆✪☆✪☆✪☆✪☆

Martin: How's business going?

Justina: I'm looking for a new secretary.

Martin: But you only had a new one last week.

Justina: Yes, that's the one I'm looking for!

☆✪☆✪☆✪☆✪☆

⊙ What did the fireman's wife get for Christmas?

Ⓐ A ladder in her stocking

☆✪☆✪☆✪☆✪☆

⊙ What do you call an American drawing?

Ⓐ A yankee doodle

☆✪☆✪☆✪☆✪☆

⊙ Why was the Egyptian girl worried?

Ⓐ Because her daddy was a mummy

☆✪☆✪☆✪☆✪☆

⊙ What's the best thing to take into the desert?

Ⓐ A thirst-aid kit!

Gag-tastic!

What do you get if you cross a toad with a galaxy?

Star warts!

☆✪☆✪☆✪☆✪☆

What does the winner of the race lose?

His breath

☆✪☆✪☆✪☆✪☆

Ryan: A noise woke me up this morning.

Katie: What was that?

Ryan: The crack of dawn!

☆✪☆✪☆✪☆✪☆

What do you get if you cross rabbits and termites?

Bugs bunnies

☆✪☆✪☆✪☆✪☆

What do you get if you cross a crocodile and a flower?

I don't know, but I wouldn't try sniffing it

Animal antics

Q What's the easiest way to count a herd of cattle?

A Use a cow-culator!

☆✪☆✪☆✪☆✪☆

Q **What's blue and has big ears?**

A **An elephant at the North Pole!**

☆✪☆✪☆✪☆✪☆

Q How do fireflies start a race?

A Ready, steady, glow!

☆✪☆✪☆✪☆✪☆

Q **What do you get if you cross a hen and a dog?**

A **Pooched eggs!**

☆✪☆✪☆✪☆✪☆

Pam: What's the difference between an elephant and a post box?

Sandra: I don't know.

Pam: Well I'm not asking you to post my letters!

☆✪☆✪☆✪☆✪☆

Q **Why did the cow cross the road?**

A **To get to the udder side!**

Mad world

What did one lift say to the other lift?

"I think I'm coming down with something!"

☆✪☆✪☆✪☆✪☆

Why can't a leopard hide?

Because he's always spotted!

☆✪☆✪☆✪☆✪☆

Doctor, Doctor, I think I'm a yo-yo

Are you stringing me along?

☆✪☆✪☆✪☆✪☆

What goes Oh, Oh, Oh?

Santa walking backwards

☆✪☆✪☆✪☆✪☆

What did Cinderella say to the photographer?

"Some day my prints will come."

☆✪☆✪☆✪☆✪☆

How do you hide an elephant in a cherry tree?

Paint his toenails red

☆✪☆✪☆✪☆✪☆

"What did you get that little medal for?"

"For singing"

"What did you get the big one for?"

"For stopping!"

Slapstick

Q What exam do young witches have to pass?

A A spell-ing test!

☆✪☆✪☆✪☆✪☆

Q What do you call a mosquito with a tin suit?

A A bite in shining armour

Julie was sitting on her daddy's lap. She gazed up at her father and said, "Daddy, did anyone ever tell you that you're the most wonderful and smartest man in the world?"
Her father, filled with pride said, "Why no, darling, they haven't."
"Then where did you get the idea?" she asked.

☆✪☆✪☆✪☆✪☆

Q What's taken before you get it?

A Your photo

☆✪☆✪☆✪☆✪☆

Q What is at the end of everything?

A The letter G

Mum: What are you doing Matthew?

Matthew: Writing my friend a letter.

Mum: That's a lovely idea, but why are you writing so slowly?

Matthew: Because he can't read very fast!

☆✪☆✪☆✪☆✪☆

Dave: I bought this computer yesterday and I found a twig in the disk drive!

Assistant: I'm sorry, Sir, you'll have to speak to the branch manager.

☆✪☆✪☆✪☆✪☆

◉ **How do bank robbers send messages?**

🅰 **By flee mail!**

◉ Why did the teacher write the lesson on the windows?

🅰 He wanted it to be very clear!

☆✪☆✪☆✪☆✪☆

Doctor, Doctor, I keep thinking I'm a dog

Sit on the couch and we'll talk about it

But I'm not allowed on the furniture!

Q Knock, knock!
Who's there?
Duey
Duey who?
turn over for answer!

What do you call...

○ What do you call a woman with a bunch of holly on her head?

Ⓐ Carol

☆✪☆✪☆✪☆✪☆

○ **What do you call a woman with a spring on her head?**

Ⓐ **April**

☆✪☆✪☆✪☆✪☆

○ **What do you call a man with scratch marks on his head?**

Ⓐ **Claude**

☆✪☆✪☆✪☆✪☆

○ What do you call a man with a car number plate on his head?

Ⓐ Reg

☆✪☆✪☆✪☆✪☆

○ **What do you call a man with a car on his head?**

Ⓐ **Jack**

☆✪☆✪☆✪☆✪☆

A Duey have to keep telling me Knock, knock jokes?

Terrible teachers

Teacher: I despair, Joe, how do you manage to get so many things wrong in a day?

Joe: Because I always get here early!

Mark: I wish we lived long ago.

Teacher: Why is that?

Mark: We wouldn't have so much history to learn.

Teacher: Why can't you ever answer any of my questions?

Bert: Well if I could there wouldn't be much point in me being here.

◉ Why did the teacher have such a high-pitched voice?

🅰 He had falsetto teeth

Teacher: What's your name?

Pupil: Fred.

Teacher: You should say "Sir".

Pupil: OK, Sir Fred!

191

Produced by Miles Kelly Publishing Ltd, Bardfield Centre,
Great Bardfield, Essex, England CM7 4SL

Produced for Advanced Marketing (UK) Ltd, Bicester, Oxon

2 4 6 8 10 9 7 5 3 1

Editorial Director
Anne Marshall

Project Management
Mark Darling

Cover Design
Debbie Meekcoms

Production
Estela Godoy

Cartoons by Martin Angel

British Library Cataloguing-in-Publication Data
A catalogue record for this book is available from the British Library

ISBN 1-90393-845-7

Printed in Singapore